Jules Verne's Scotland

Jules Verne's Scotland
In fact and fiction

There is only one country that was given by
God! It is Scotland to the Scottish.
Jules Verne, *Sans dessus dessous*, 1889

IAN THOMPSON

Luath Press Limited
EDINBURGH
www.luath.co.uk

First published 2011

ISBN: 978 1 906817 37 4

The publisher acknowledges subsidy from

towards the publication of this book

The paper used in this book is sourced from renewable forestry
and is FSC credited material.

Printed and bound by
MPG Books Ltd., Cornwall

Maps © Mike Shand

Typeset in 11 point Sabon
by 3btype.com

Cover images: sketch of Jules Verne reading proofs: © National Portrait Gallery;
the RMS *Columba* moored at Ardrishaig for passengers to connect with the
Crinan Canal: courtesy University of Aberdeen Library

Author photograph: Les Hill

Jules Verne (front flap): from Jules Claretie's 'Jules Verne', Paris 1883.
Courtesy of the Trustees of the National Library of Scotland

Contents

LIST OF FIGURES

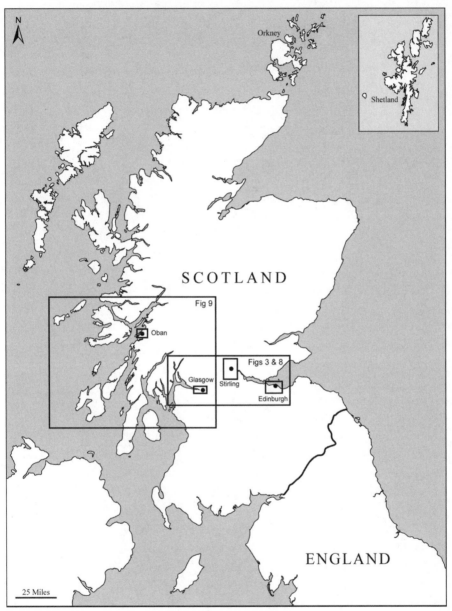

FIG. 1 Location of maps

Acknowledgements

THANKS ARE DUE TO a large number of individuals and institutions for help and encouragement in the preparation of this book. Amongst 'Vernians' special thanks are due to the late Zvi Har El for access to the Jules Verne Forum, an invaluable source of feedback via this website. Philippe Valetoux provided me with information on Verne's second journey to Scotland derived from Verne's *carnets de voyages* and Piero Gondolo della Riva similarly with documentary evidence with respect to the 1859 journey. William Butcher, Geoff Woollen and Tim Unwin gave encouragement especially at the very early stages of my interest in Verne and Scotland. Marie Buckley and other residents kindly gave access to Inzievar House, while Kari Petrie and Marianne Chalmers gave assistance with the family histories of the Smith-Sligo and Bain families respectively. At the Department of Geographical and Earth Sciences at the University of Glasgow, Yvonne Finlayson and Les Hill provided help with illustrative material while Mike Shand lent his outstanding cartographic talents. Among the institutions that have given direct help, thanks are due to staff at the National Library of Scotland, especially Yvonne Shand, the National Archives of Scotland, especially Leanne Swallow, the Royal Commission on the Ancient and Historical Monuments Scotland, especially Dr Miles Oglethorpe, and staff at the Mitchell Library, Glasgow. At Glasgow University Library, grateful thanks are due to staff at the Special Collections, especially the Keeper, David Westen, and at the Business Archives, George Gardner. The Carnegie Library, Dunfermline and the William Patrick Library, Kirkintilloch provided helpful local detail. Thanks are due to Edinburgh Central Library, especially Mr James Hogg, for provision of 19th century photographs of Edinburgh. On transport issues, the Ships of Calmac Society, particularly Steve Hurst, and David Blevens, and David Hinds of the Caledonian Railway Association, provided clarification of rail transport issues. Dr Robert McCulloch provided valuable information on the demise of the original Caledonian Hotel in Oban. Kerr Doig and Sheila Pitcairn of Dunfermline City Archives helped with local detail in the Oakley area. In England, Douglas Herdson, Information Officer at the

National Marine Aquarium, Plymouth, gave information on the range of the Hammerhead Shark. Emma Butterfield of the National Portrait Gallery in London facilitated access to a previously unpublished portrait of Verne and Anne Crowne, of Lloyds Yacht Register, gave permission to include the entry of the *St-Michel III*. At Aberdeen University, Kim Downie aided the reproduction of images from the Washington Wilson Collection. Thanks are also due to Valerie Boa, Curator of the McLean Museum and Art Gallery, Greenock, for permission to reproduce an image of the RMS *Columba*. In France, Professeur Jean Bastié, President of the Société de Géographie, facilitated access to the archives of the Society and M. Alain Marquer arranged consultation of the archives of the *Alliance Française* in Paris, of which Verne was a founder member. M. Bernard Sinoquet, Curator of the Verne Collection at La Bibliothèque Centrale d'Amiens permitted consultation of the *carnets de voyages* of Verne's 1879 visit to Scotland. I am grateful to the Strathmartine Trust for funding archival visits to France.

Above all, I am grateful to Gavin MacDougall, Managing Director of Luath Press, for his support for this and other Jules Verne projects.

Ian Thompson

Prologue

TOWARDS MIDNIGHT ON Friday 26 August 1859, the Caledonian Railway express train from Carlisle pulled into Edinburgh's spartan Lothian Road Terminus. As the smoke and steam cleared, two figures emerged on the platform. One was a musician, Aristide Hignard. The other was his friend, Jules Verne, then aged 31. For Verne, setting foot on Scotland's soil was the realisation of a dream, for he claimed descent on his mother's side from a 15th century Scot, Allott, who had enlisted in the Scottish regiment of King Louis XI of France. With the creation of the Auld Alliance signed in Dunfermline in 1296, essentially a military alliance against England, it was not uncommon for Scottish mercenaries to serve in the French Army. After loyal service, Allott was ennobled and assumed the title of Allotte de la Fuÿe, signifying the substantial privilege of owning a dovecote on his land. From boyhood, Jules Verne had revelled in his Scottish connection, further enhanced by his passion for the works of Sir Walter Scott, which he had read in translation since he had no competence whatever in the English language. In an interview given in 1895, he pointed to the well-worn copies of Scott's books in his library and stated:

> All my life I have delighted in the works of Sir Walter Scott, and during a never-to-be-forgotten tour in the British Isles, my happiest days were spent in Scotland. I still see, as in a vision, beautiful picturesque Edinburgh, with its Heart of Midlothian, and many entrancing memories; the Highlands, world-forgotten Iona, and the wild Hebrides. Of course, to one familiar with the works of Scott, there is scarce a district of his native land lacking some association connected with the writer and his immortal work.[1]

Although Verne had boundless pride in his distant Scottish ancestry, it is unlikely that he would have visited Scotland and produced his Scottish books without the inspiration of Scott's works .

Having been born a Breton, albeit on the extreme south-east margin of Brittany, Verne had an instinctive empathy with Celtic nations, which he regarded as being subdued by more powerful neighbours. Thus Scotland and Ireland evoked his sympathy and provided fertile ground for his creative imagination.

Verne's arrival in Edinburgh was more than just his first journey abroad. Having been born in Nantes and struggled to achieve a literary career in Paris, it was his first encounter with lakes and mountains as immortalised in the writings and paintings of the Romantic Movement. In fact, in correspondence and writing, he mentioned his visit to 'the Scottish Lakes', referring primarily to Loch Lomond and Loch Katrine. It was the fulfilment of his ambition to set foot in 'his' Scotland, the land of his ancestors. Moreover, he had acquired a vast compendium of knowledge of Scotland, especially its history, from voracious reading which he was now to transform into first-hand experience.

This first visit to Scotland was brief, a mere five days, but it was sufficient to instil in him a love of the country and its people which was to be sustained throughout his life. It was to inspire a travelogue and five novels set entirely or partly in Scotland. Moreover, countless Scottish characters populate his other books. They range from aristocrats to simple seamen, rich businessmen to modest servants, all characterised by qualities of loyalty, endurance and fortitude. The female characters display charm and intelligence but no lack of determination.

After this first visit, Verne returned to Scotland 20 years later in 1879. By then, having achieved fame and relative fortune, Verne arrived not by train, a struggling and unknown writer, but as a world famous author sailing into the port of Leith in his own handsome steam yacht with a crew of ten. Berthing his yacht, Verne not only revisited his favourite haunts in Edinburgh, The Trossachs and Loch Lomond, but by train and steamer extended his travels in Scotland to Argyll, Oban and the islands of Mull, Iona and Staffa. His Scottish novels therefore span Verne's personality from excitable but frustrated and unfulfilled young man to successful author, with sufficient wealth to travel in style and comfort in early middle age.

My decision to write this book sprang from the fact that very few people with whom I had discussed Verne had any idea that he had both visited Scotland and used this experience to write books set in the country. This may be a result of the language barrier, since modern high quality English translations of some of his Scottish novels have only recently appeared. Accordingly references to material in French have largely been omitted but can easily be accessed by consulting appropriate biographies and collections recommended at the close of the work. This book therefore chronicles Verne's travels in Scotland, his impressions and experiences, and demonstrates the influence that this had on the writing of his 'Scottish' novels. It is thus an account of Jules Verne's Scotland, in fact and fiction.

Ian Thompson, Glasgow 2011

Note

1   Belloc, M, 'Jules Verne at home', *Strand Magazine*, February 1895.

PART ONE

Scotland Visited

CHAPTER ONE

First Impressions, 1859

JULES VERNE WAS BORN in the French city of Nantes, at the head of the estuary of the Loire on the south-east margin of Brittany, on 8 February, 1828. His father was a successful lawyer who anticipated that Jules, as the elder son, would in the fullness of time inherit the practice. This intention was never fulfilled, for at an early age Jules viewed such a prosaic profession as being utterly incompatible with his imaginative and romantic nature. These qualities were enhanced in his childhood by the bustle of the port on the River Loire, with its vessels trading with far-off and exotic sounding countries.

The port of Nantes, and indeed the city's bourgeoisie, had thrived on the slave trade and colonial commerce. It was thus no ordinary port that entranced the young Jules, for its vessels traded with distant lands and in exotic products. In addition it was one of France's major whaling ports. This was a heady mix for a young boy with an overactive imagination. Before Jules had reached the age of ten, his father rented a substantial summer residence in Chantenay, at that time a rural commune on the north bank of the Loire to the west of Nantes. The young Jules and his brother Paul spent magical times there for the property overlooked the Loire, a tempestuous river flooding the adjacent meadows in winter and reduced to braided channels between sandbanks when the river level fell during the summer. He had a grandstand view not only of the shipping, but also the huge factories on the river banks. The foundries of Indret-sur-Mer and the Basse-Indre factory produced marine components from anchors and chains to the metal forgings for shipbuilding. Jules gaped at the monstrous machines, and the almost nightmarish power of modern technology induced in him a fascination with industrial production and its potential for both good and ill, which was to be reflected decades later in his writing. [FIG. 2]

He grew up in this nautical wonderland and dreamed of voyaging himself. This yearning to explore the world's oceans was further excited by the tales of an uncle, a retired sea captain, who lived in the countryside south of the Loire[1]. The summer holidays were often spent at his home

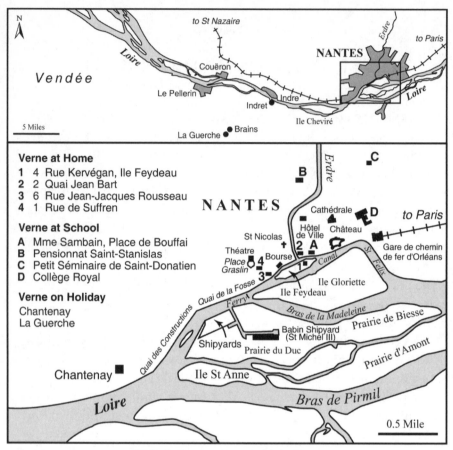

FIG. 2 Nantes, Verne's birthplace

and in addition to regaling Jules with his seafaring adventures, his uncle also repeatedly reminded him of his Scottish ancestry. Alas for Jules it was his younger brother Paul who was allowed to join the merchant navy while he, at least in his father's mind, was destined for the legal profession. Given his day-dreams of faraway lands reached by daring sea captains, and his determination that one day he too would sail the seas in search of adventure, a more unsuitable candidate for the life of a provincial lawyer is difficult to imagine.

At school, Jules was a satisfactory if not brilliant scholar who showed particular promise in literature, music and geography, all of which were to be the backbone of his adult creative life. On leaving senior school, after a short period of apprenticeship in the family practice in Nantes, Jules was enrolled in the Law Faculty in Paris in 1848 aged 20 as a necessary step towards joining the family legal practice. Such a fate could not have been further from Jules' mind for he was determined to follow a literary career. To the grief of his father, Jules spent his time on the fringe of the literary and theatrical milieu in relative poverty, writing a prolific amount of short plays and *libretti* for operettas and working briefly as a theatre secretary. Although he made the acquaintance of several major literary figures, his own work was largely unsuccessful and did not provide him with a livelihood. He spent entire days in public libraries reading and making notes in comfort and warmth as opposed to his cold garret apartment. He dined regularly with a group of ten other unmarried young men, but as one by one they succumbed to matrimony, Jules himself began to fret for a wife, and preferably a wealthy one. In spite of his impecunious position, he never lost faith in his own destiny to be a famous author, and although he gained his law degree, his parents had to accept that he would never succeed his father in the family practice and that his literary ambitions tied him to Paris.

It was at this stage in 1856 that, when attending the wedding in Amiens of one of his friends, he met and was enamoured of a young woman of 26, Honorine Deviane. Already a widow with two young daughters, Verne courted her and marriage followed in January 1857, the match being eased on Verne's part by the fact that Honorine had a substantial dowry. In spite of his wife's resources, which enabled the newly-weds and their daughters to settle into more comfortable accommodation in Paris, Verne went through the motions of working for a living as a dealer in a bank. If the truth be known, his appearances at the bank were far from regular and the urge to write still dominated his psyche. It was at this stage, in 1859, that his dream of seeing Scotland became a reality.

His school friend Aristide Hignard, like Verne, had settled in Paris; he launched a musical career and they shared a similar circle of acquaintances. Hignard's brother Alfred was a shipping agent who regularly chartered vessels exporting French cargoes to Britain. He was able to offer Aristide free passage on a steamer sailing from St-Nazaire, at the mouth of the Loire, headed for Liverpool. Hignard invited Verne to accompany him and he immediately accepted. His excited correspondence with his parents shows that Liverpool was not his intended destination but merely a stepping stone en route for Scotland!

The journey to Liverpool was not without complications. The sailing schedule was changed and the two friends were obliged to sail from Nantes to Bordeaux and wait for several days until the arrival of the British steamship, the SS *Hamburg*. In effect, they had set off in the opposite direction to their intended destination and hence when Verne's account of their journey was published it was entitled *Voyage à reculons en Angleterre et en Ecosse*[2], which was subsequently translated into English as *Backwards to Britain*[3]. In fact this book is the main source of information on Verne's first visit to Scotland. It is written in a lively and humorous style and is no doubt a little embroidered and lightly fictionalised. Nevertheless, it is possible to verify much of the content and to establish that it is in fact an authentic autobiographical account. Verne disguised his identity in the book by adopting the name of 'Jacques Lavaret' while Hignard became 'Jonathan Savournon'.

It is important to understand what kind of man, at age 31, was to land on the shore of Britain for the first time. Certainly, as we know from a letter written to his father dated 15 July 1859, Verne was excited by the prospect of visiting Scotland;

> In a week or so, I've got a chance to go to Nantes, alone this time... Alfred Hignard has offered his brother and me a free trip to Scotland and back on one of his ships. So I'm grabbing the chance to make such a lovely trip.

His young wife of only two years was left behind to join family in her home town of Amiens while Verne set off on his adventure; a precedent for future negligence including his absence in Copenhagen at the birth of his only son in August 1861. This is one of many examples of Verne's paradoxical character. He was extremely well-educated, both as a result of his rigorous school studies to obtain his *baccalauréat* and his somewhat unenthusiastic legal studies in Paris. But arguably Verne owed his remarkable intellectual versatility and polymath erudition to his own efforts. From youth he had been an avid reader of fiction and had also composed poems on a variety of topics, ranging from bitter recriminations due to unrequited romance to wicked humorous parodies and double entendre of an explicit nature. If Walter Scott had inspired his passion for Scotland, he was also a devoted admirer of Charles Dickens, whose vivid evocation of urban poverty was confirmed by his own observations in the poorer parts of Liverpool, Edinburgh, Glasgow and London. He also appreciated James Fenimore Cooper and Edgar Allan Poe, who inspired his later novels set in America. His zest for literature was accompanied by a passionate interest in music and he was an accomplished pianist. In his early years in Paris he had devoured the contents of libraries, making copious notes carefully classified for future reference. Equally important, he had mingled with both the literary and scientific milieus in Paris and had absorbed all that this had to offer. By the time he set sail Verne was thus a sophisticated and ambitious young man, convinced of his vocation to be a famous author, but as yet unrecognised and financially insecure. His one practical deficiency was a lack of modern foreign languages, his education having been based on the classical languages.

His intellectual resources were, however, not entirely matched by an equivalent experience of social conditions. Although in Paris he was far from unaware of the seamier aspects of urban living, his bourgeois family background had sheltered him from exposure to the scale of squalor and poverty that he was to witness in the docks area of Liverpool, the pestilential courtyards of Edinburgh or the overcrowded and unhygienic quarters of the old town in Glasgow. He thus arrived in Scotland with a head full of romantic images, gleaned from Sir Walter Scott and the Celtic legends, but his eyes were opened when he was confronted with the less congenial side of urban life in mid-19th century Scotland.

Ashore in Britain

After a three day journey from Bordeaux, the ss *Hamburg* docked in Liverpool at 5am on 25 August. Verne was astonished at the scale of the port at Liverpool, which dwarfed that of his home city of Nantes. The docks extended as far as the eye could see and the density of the moored vessels almost obscured the water.

In spite of the squalor, violence and ugliness that he witnessed in Liverpool, Verne remained attached to the city and stated that it was the English city he knew best. He was to revisit it in 1867 with his brother Paul, en route to New York aboard Brunel's gigantic *Great Eastern*, which inspired his book *Une ville flottante*, 1869, (*A Floating City*) and he sited the opening of one of his best known novels, *Voyages et aventures du capitaine Hatteras*, 1866, (*The Adventures of Captain Hatteras*) in the port of Liverpool[4]. In fact Verne later expressed the opinion that the port was superior to that of Glasgow, in spite of the latter being Scottish!

After lunch on 26 August, the companions made their way to Liverpool Lime Street railway station, the terminus of the London and North Western Railway, to board the express to Edinburgh[5]. The train would have been hauled by a steam-powered cable up the steep incline from the station through the long tunnel to Edge Hill. Verne admired the speed of the train, which exceeded that of French railways, but had some concern for its safety. This was a shrewd observation since the speed of the express was not accompanied by adequate braking power, especially when running on steep downhill gradients. The locomotive was probably a 2-2-2 Cornwall class, its giant single driving wheel accounting for its rapid speed across the level plains of central Lancashire. Passing through Wigan and Preston, the express continued along the main line from London and headed north through Lancaster to reach Carlisle. Here the Caledonian Railway carriages would have been detached and taken over by a handsome Caledonian engine. Given that the Carlisle to Scotland route was the Caledonian Railway Company's prestige run, it is likely that the locomotive would have been the company's latest acquisition, the brand new Connor 2-2-2, with massive eight feet two inch driving wheels. Soon after leaving Carlisle, to Verne's great excitement, the train crossed the border at Gretna. Verne's spirits rose further as the train threaded its way through the hills of the Southern Uplands, which in Verne's eyes were 'mountains', to reach Carstairs. Here the train split, with the front coaches continuing to Glasgow and the rear ones branching eastwards to Edinburgh. The Edinburgh coaches were hauled by an older and smaller 2-2-2 engine. The combination of excitement and fatigue proved too much for the pair and as darkness enclosed the train they fell fast asleep for the last stage of the journey.

Scotland at last! – Arrival in 'Auld Reekie'

Disembarking from the train in pouring rain around midnight at Caledonian's unprepossessing terminus at Lothian Road[6], the pair hailed a cab and ordered the coachman to take them to Lambré's Hotel, 18 Princes Street. The hotel was owned by a Frenchman, Nicolas Lambré, and had possibly been recommended to them or discovered in a French guide book[7]. Exhausted and ravenous after their long journey from Liverpool, they ate cold meat washed down with two pints of frothing ale before retiring at one o'clock. The subsequent travels of Verne and Hignard in 1859 are summarised in FIG. 3.

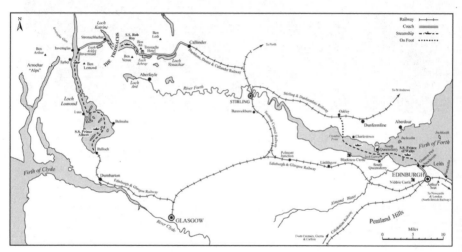

FIG. 3 The 1859 itinerary

Although spending only three days in the city, by dint of continuous exploration on foot, by horse-drawn omnibus and carriage, they witnessed the essence of mid-19th century Edinburgh. By 1859 the essential features of the core of the city had been established. For centuries it had been a 'one street town' along the hilltop axis of the High Street. This 'Royal Mile', rich in historical and literary associations, made a deep impression on Verne. Built on the steep-sided ridge from the Castle to Holyrood Palace, the confined site imposed a very high density of buildings, often ten storeys high, and a lack of open space other than the street itself. The congested and animated street, except on Sundays as Verne was to discover

The view of Edinburgh's Old Town from Lambré's Hotel in 1859.
In the foreground is the General Railway Station and in the background,
the 'skyscraper' tenements lining the High Street.
City of Edinburgh Council

to his cost, resonated with him more than the magnificent monumental public buildings, which he almost ignored. For Verne it was the throbbing life of the street itself, the skyscraper tenements and dingy noisome back closes of the Canongate, the coffee houses and taverns, the scenes evoked by Walter Scott, that most captured his imagination.

Edinburgh's New Town, developed from the mid-18th century onwards, seems to have interested him less, other than the vista it afforded across the Princes Street Gardens to the Old Town and to Arthur's Seat. The geometrical layout of streets and squares, and above all the pseudo Grecian High School building and the 'reproduction' monuments on Calton Hill were regarded with disdain.

In particular Verne disparaged the Nelson Monument. In *Backwards to Britain* he states;

At the top of the hill stands the Nelson Monument which is of great height and topped by a signal for the ships that sail up and down the Forth. This tower has a dismal shape and is so inelegant it is painful to contemplate.

Backwards to Britain (Chapter 25)

For Verne, the New Town lacked the colour and bustle of the Old Town. It was a bourgeois domain of wealth and privilege as compared with the social warp and weft of the High Street.

At this time, Edinburgh was in rapid expansion, the city itself housing over 160,000 inhabitants and beginning to merge physically with the adjacent settlements on the coast and inland. Verne was to witness this spread at first hand. In his visit to Lauriston he saw a prototype inner suburb being created for the burgeoning business and professional classes. At the seaside resort of Portobello, he observed growth resulting from the recreational demand of an urban population and its hinterland. By contrast, Granton and Newhaven represented the absorption into the agglomeration of specialised 'villages', a ferry port and fishing village respectively. In comparison, Leith was a substantial port and provided Edinburgh with a maritime outlet to the North Sea.

Edinburgh explored

At the first light of dawn on 27 August, Verne could contain his excitement no longer and threw open the window of his room and peered over the balcony. His eyes feasted on the animation of Princes Street and across the gardens to the Old Town with its castle surmounting the crag and tenements lining the crest of the hill. His gaze scoured the horizon and lighted on the extinct volcano of Arthur's Seat, which he declared to Hignard would be their immediate ascension. The less impetuous Hignard demurred and insisted that their first exploration would be the Old Town and to defer climbing the summit until fortified by a hearty lunch.

To follow the itinerary of the two friends in Edinburgh and throughout the remainder of their stay in Scotland, it is essential to read *Backwards to Britain*, especially to appreciate Verne's reaction to the sights and sounds, but also to enjoy some of the comic episodes he describes and which were almost certainly invented. Here, we will concentrate on those aspects of

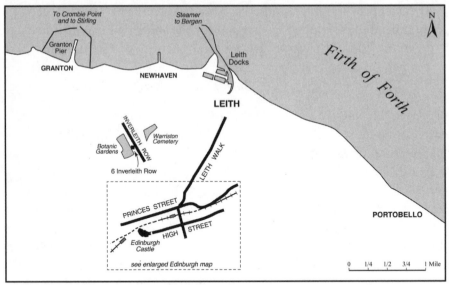

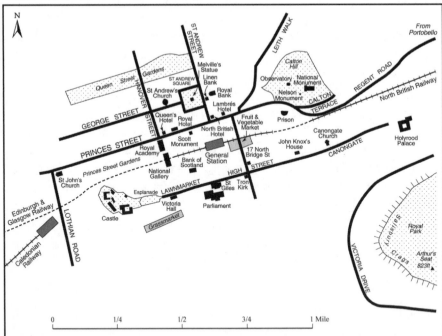

FIG. 4 Jules Verne's Edinburgh

his journey which were to sum up his experience of Scotland and which were to provide him with material and ideas for his Scottish novels. FIG. 4 indicates the locations in Edinburgh named by Verne in *Backwards to Britain* and in his subsequent novels.

On leaving their hotel, the companions retraced the steps of the previous evening by strolling along Princes Street to Lothian Road. They admired Scott's Memorial, the Royal Academy, the gardens and the general harmony of the buildings. Deciding to take a circular route around the Castle Rock, they climbed up to the Grassmarket and gained the High Street near St Giles' Cathedral. Strangely, the Castle did not hold their attention nor were they impressed by St Giles, an example of 'heavy' Anglo-Saxon Gothic, nor Parliament House. These architectural reservations were, however, offset by Verne's identification of the locales of scenes from Scott's *The Heart of Midlothian*.

> On reading *The Heart of Midlothian*, Jacques [Verne] had developed an archaeological passion for the old Tolbooth, where poor Effie Deans was imprisoned and suffered so bitterly. He had studied that part of the novel carefully and intended to show off his knowledge; by now he reckoned they should have reached the sinister prison.
>
> *Backwards to Britain* (Chapter 19)

Passing John Knox's House, they paused for lunch in a tavern near the Tron Kirk[8] before continuing their traverse of the Old Town towards the Palace of Holyrood. Following the Canongate, the pair encountered the ugly side of the city.

> The area that leads to the royal palace is one of utter misery. Naked children, barefoot women and girls dressed in rags, beggars with hats, jostle, pass, drag themselves along and slink past the tall tenements with their pinched, starved features. And yet, in the middle of that abject populace, in the foul, diseased-ridden atmosphere, on the muddy pavement and down those dark, dank horrid lanes or closes which lead to revolting slums, slithering down stepless ramps towards the ravines on either side of the Canongate, one is gripped by the terrible poetry of old Scotland!
>
> *Backwards to Britain* (Chapter 20)

Verne's favourite Edinburgh street, the High Street, looking towards the Canongate. This view dates from Verne's second visit in 1879 and features the supposed house of John Knox, close to which was the fictional residence of the Reverend Tyrcomel in *The Fabulous Adventures of Master Antifer* (1894).
City of Edinburgh Council

Relief from this depressing spectacle was provided by the broadening of the Canongate as Holyrood Palace was approached. In fact Holyrood impressed Verne less as a building than as the scene of dramatic and tragic historical events and his eyes continued to be drawn to the summit of Arthur's Seat. Verne made straight for the Salisbury Crags, followed by a struggling Hignard. The strenuous climb to the summit was rewarded by a panorama which took Verne's breath away.

> The whole city was spread out below, with the modern districts and regular streets of the New Town contrasting with *Auld Reekie's* confused tangle of houses and crazy network of alleys. Two land-marks dominated the skyline, the Castle on its basalt rock, and Calton Hill, with the ruins of a Greek temple on its rounded summit. Splendid tree-lined avenues converged on the capital. To the north, an arm of the sea, the Firth of Forth with the Port of Leith at its mouth, cut deeply inland. North of the Firth lay the

Holyrood Palace

Holyrood Palace and Arthur's Seat. Salisbury Crags are visible on the right.
The view from the summit was one of Verne's most enduring memories.
Anonymous postcard

harmonious coastline of the kingdom of Fife; to the east stretched
the boundless expanse of sea which always looks blue and calm
when viewed from such heights. A road as straight as the one to
Piraeus linked this new Athens to the North Sea, as Charles Nodier
observed. The distant peak of Ben Lomond was visible to the west
and below, to the right of Arthur's Seat, stretched out the beaches of
Newhaven and Portobello, with their bathing resorts. No pen can
do justice to this breathtaking scene.

Backwards to Britain (Chapter 20)[9]

Verne was so overwhelmed by the spectacular panorama that he was to
exploit it twice more in his novels. However exciting the view Verne was
determined to press on with their exploration and the aerial view of the
coast guided their descent to Portobello. At this time an active resort,
the beach was thronged with bathers and in spite of having no bathing
suits the two friends plunged naked into the chilly sea and then rushed
back to the security and modesty of their changing cabin. Exhausted by
the ascension of Arthur's Seat and by their swim, they repaired to a

seafront inn and restored themselves with a glass of ale. A horse-drawn omnibus took them past the prison and beneath Calton Hill to the New Town. Here they descended and retraced their steps to Lambré's Hotel to rest and to consult a map, for a further excursion awaited them. Hignard's brother had married the niece of a Scottish businessman, a certain Mr B who lived in the New Town, and it was sure that a warm welcome awaited them at his house. Accordingly they set off in the direction of Leith, crossing the handsome squares and town houses of the New Town until they reached Inverleith Row. At that time, this impressive avenue was in the course of development. Bisecting the Botanic Gardens to the west and Lauriston Cemetery to the east, it was a fitting district for a bourgeois family.

Verne disguised the name of Mr B, the original manuscript blotting out all but the capital letter of the surname. However, by a variety of means we can identify him as William Bain, Manager of the Edinburgh Branch of the City of Glasgow Bank. This conclusion is reached by an examination of *Slater's Directory of Scotland* for 1859, which reveals no other surname beginning with 'B' resident in Inverleith Row. Moreover, the description of the house provided by Verne corresponds exactly with number 6 Inverleith Row identified in the Directory, with a front and rear garden and a location at the entry to the Botanic Gardens and opposite the entry to Warriston Cemetery. The Census of 1861 indicates the Bain family as residing in a fourteen apartment house with five children and two resident servants[10].

Verne and Hignard were admitted by a maid to the first floor drawing room of the Bain house where they met Mrs Bain and her daughter Margaret, who Verne disguises as 'Amelia' in *Backwards to Britain*. At the time of their visit, she would have been almost 18 and Verne was immediately smitten both by her charm and her fluent French, spoken with a fetching Scottish accent. As Mr B was not at home, the companions were invited to stay to dinner and in the meantime Margaret proposed a walk in the neighbourhood, to which they immediately agreed. They promenaded in the Botanic Gardens, created some 40 years earlier and thus offering a mature landscape of lawns and trees. The magnificent rotunda hothouse was filled with tropical plants and its balcony provided a magnificent view over the city. After spending an hour walking and in conversation, Amelia led them across Inverleith Row to Warriston Cemetery. To his surprise

Verne found this far from mournful. As compared with the gloom of French mausoleums, this newly-created cemetery, with its neat paths, box hedges, view of the Dean valley and of the city skyline, delighted Verne.

It was just a short step across the road back to 6 Inverleith Row and the two friends were ushered into the presence of William Bain and a Catholic priest whom Verne identifies as the 'Reverend Mr S', and who was also to be a dinner guest. In fact the priest was William Smith, the 39-year-old brother of a wealthy property and mine owner, Archibald Smith, who in addition to a handsome town house with nine servants in Drummond Square in Edinburgh's New Town, had recently built a baronial mansion in Fife on his estate, close to his coal mine and ironworks at Oakley. The 1861 Census defines William Smith as a 'Catholic priest without a parish'

William Smith who Verne referred to as 'The Reverend Mr S' in *Backwards to Britain* shown here in his vestments as Archbishop of Edinburgh and St Andrews.

Studio Portrait acquired by the Trustees of the National Library of Scotland

although archives show that, for a short time at least, he served the parish of St Margaret in Dunfermline. He also had the official status of Chaplain to the wife of Archibald Smith, the former Lady Harris. To secure this appointment, she had promised the Bishop of Edinburgh that she would finance the construction of a chapel in Oakley. No doubt this was nepotism, but also a service to the Catholic community of Oakley which was without a local place of worship. He was later to rise through the Catholic hierarchy to become Archbishop of the St Andrews and Edinburgh diocese in 1878, and died in office in 1892[11]. He was buried in St Mary's Cathedral in Edinburgh.

Conversation at dinner turned towards the travel plans of the two Frenchmen. Verne was adamant that their short visit would not be complete without seeing the mountains and that his earnest wish was to see

Highlanders in their 'native' dress. The Reverend Smith exclaimed that nothing could be simpler and that his brother's castle would make an excellent starting point for a short excursion. At Amelia's urging the two agreed and she promised to draw up an itinerary that would give them an excellent taste of the Highlands. After a copious meal washed down by sherry, port and ale, followed by a rum toddy, and in spite of their tiredness, Verne and Hignard agreed to take a further walk. Mr and Mrs Bain, together with Amelia, guided them up Inverleith Row as far as the fishing village of Newhaven. It was low tide and the view of the sea across mud-flats was far from attractive. William Bain pointed out the harbour of Granton to the west from which their steamer for Stirling would sail on the following Monday for the first leg of their Highland odyssey.

The stroll back to the Bain's house was followed by another substantial 'tea'. Verne discovered that he and Hignard shared a love of music and song with Amelia and so the evening closed with songs at the piano. Amelia introduced them to Highland melodies to which the pair replied with extracts from operettas which resounded around the house. The following day being Sunday, William Bain offered to guide the friends on an afternoon walk in the city and it was agreed that they would meet at 1pm near Pitt the Younger's statue on George Street. Verne and Hignard dragged themselves wearily back to Lambré's Hotel, utterly exhausted by the day's exertions.

Refreshed after a good night's sleep, the two friends set out again in the morning determined to continue their exploration of the city. They were drawn towards the strange edifices atop Calton Hill. Verne had mixed feelings about the reproduction classic monuments and positively hated the Nelson tower, while he thought that the High School resembled a reproduction Grecian Temple. It appears that Verne lacked compre-hension of the significance of the architecture and the function of the monument. The shape of the tower resembles a telescope, recalling the event in the battle of Copenhagen when Nelson deliberately put his telescope to his blind eye, lost in the siege of Calvi in Corsica, so as to disobey the order to withdraw from the sea battle. The signal was remarkable in that precisely at 12 noon, and one o'clock in summer, a huge ball descended from the top of the tower. As the tower is over a 100 feet tall and Calton Hill is 406 feet high, the signal was visible from the port of Leith and the anchorage in the Forth estuary. This enabled

Calton Hill with Edinburgh General Station in the foreground. The Nelson
Monument, that Verne disliked, is visible on the summit.
George Washington Wilson Collection, University of Aberdeen

seamen to set their chronometers, essential for navigation at that time.
In fact, the visibility of this signal made it more accurate than the one
o'clock gun traditionally fired from Edinburgh Castle, since there was a
time lag of approximately ten seconds for the sound of the gun to reach
the port of Leith. Verne was thus too dismissive of both the probable
symbolism of the monument and its vital function for seafarers. The
monument is currently being restored to its original function.

By now, pangs of hunger drove their thoughts towards lunch and
they decided to revisit the tavern near the Tron church on the High
Street. At once, the reality of the Scottish Sunday struck them. The
streets were deserted, the shops closed and worse still, their tavern was
firmly locked and barred. In a bad temper they returned to their hotel
which mercifully served them a full lunch. It was now time to meet Mr
Bain who led them to Princes Street Gardens where, after resting on a
bench, they began the climb up to the Lawnmarket and the Castle
esplanade. By now fatigue was beginning to overcome the Frenchmen.

They just saw the outside courts but were too tired to enter the Castle and see the Scottish Crown Jewels. Verne begged his host that they might take a cab back to Inverleith Row and they duly caught one on Princes Street.

Once more they dined with the Bains and Amelia busied herself with drawing up an exact itinerary with dates, times and methods of transport. Miraculously, Verne's transcription of this document has survived and is the only direct archival evidence of Verne's first Scottish visit, consisting of a small fragment that has been folded in four as if to fit into a wallet, [FIG. 5]. The reverse of the document carries the title in Verne's hand 'First Voyage in Scotland'. It was discovered by the great Italian Verne collector Count Piero Gondolo della Riva and now resides in the Municipal Library of Amiens, which acquired his immense Verne collection[12]. A translation of this document is as follows:

Monday
1   A cab to drive us to Granton at 9.30
2   Take the steamer which leaves for Sterling [sic] at 10.30
3   Arrive at **Cromby(sic)-point** (chez Mr Smith)
4   Leave in the evening for **Glasgow** at 4 from Oakley, arrive at Sterling at 5.10 leave again and arrive at Glasgow at 7.10

Tuesday
1   Leave Glasgow at 10.45 by the railway
2   Arrive at **Balloch** at 12.00
3   Leave Balloch by the steamer at 12.20 (beginning of Loch Lomond) and arrive at **Inversnaid (close to the loch)**
4   Disembark at Inversnaid at 2.10 – ask for a coach or walk the 4 miles to **Stronochlachar** (beginning of Loch Katrine) at 3.10
5   At 3.30 the boat leaves, crosses the lake and arrives at **Trossachs**, at the end of Loch Katrine
6   At Trossachs find a coach to take us to Sterling for the last train to **Edinburgh**

Sterling to Edinburgh 8.10–9.50

At 10pm goodnights were exchanged and the pair made their way back to their hotel for their final night in Edinburgh.

After the pleasant weather of the last two days, Tuesday dawned

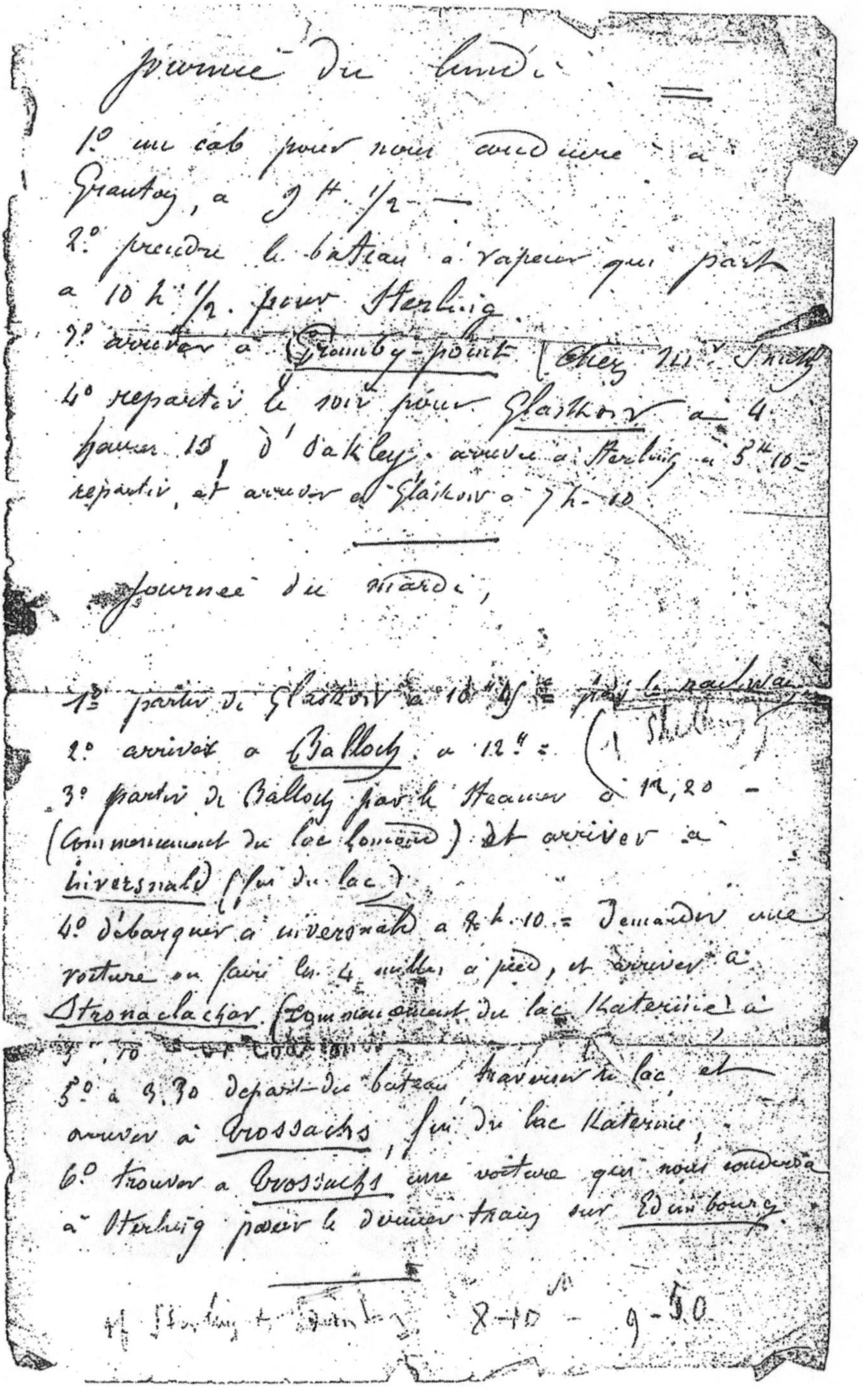
Journée du lundi

1° un cab pour nous conduire à
Granton, à 9 h. 1/2 —
2° prendre le bateau à vapeur qui part
à 10 h 1/2. pour Sterling.
3° arriver à Granby-point (chez Mr Smith)
4° repartir le soir pour Glasgow à 4
heures 10, d'Oakley. arriver à Sterling à 5 h 10 =
repartir, et arriver à Glasgow à 7 h. 10.

Journée du mardi,

1° partir de Glasgow à 10 h 45 par le railway
2° arriver à Balloch à 12 h = (1 Shilling)
3° partir de Balloch par le steamer à 12,20 —
(commencement du lac Lomond) et arriver à
Inversnaid (fin du lac)
4° débarquer à Inversnaid à 2 h. 10. = Demander une
voiture ou faire les 4 milles à pied, et arriver à
Stronaclachar (commencement du lac Katerine) à
3 h. 10
5° à 3.30 départ du bateau traverser le lac, et
arriver à Trossachs, fin du lac Katerine,
6° trouver à Trossachs une voiture qui nous conduira
à Sterling pour le dernier train sur Edinbourg.

8-40 — 9-50

FIG. 5 The only known document of the 1859 Scottish journey.

with lashing rain and a strong wind. After breakfasting with the Bain family and leaving their surplus baggage at their house, at 9am a cab deposited them at Granton Pier where they boarded the Stirling steamship, the *Prince of Wales*, which was to transport them on the next stage of their Scottish adventure[13]. Thus ended Verne's first visit to Edinburgh, a sojourn which he had found exhilarating and which he was to return to both in person and in his storytelling.

Headed for the Highlands

On leaving the shelter of the harbour, the *Prince of Wales* headed into the teeth of the gale. We can verify Verne's account of the weather by reference to the *Edinburgh Evening Courant* for 30 August, which reported strong south-west winds and rain on the previous day. Verne's steamer would have been sailing into a strong side to head wind and lashed by rain. After this experience, he decided that their return journey to France via London would be by rail rather than by sea! Nevertheless, Verne could

Crombie Point, Fife. In the foreground is Black Anchor Tavern where the Reverend Mr Smith took Verne and Hignard for a whisky. It is now a private dwelling.
National Archives of Scotland (Erskine Beveridge Collection)

identify the landmarks as the steamer made its unsteady way westwards up the Firth of Forth[14]. In turn Aberdour, Queensferry, Rosyth, Blackness Castle and Charlestown were passed with Verne reciting to Hignard the historical events associated with them[15]. A dramatic moment occurred as they neared their destination of Crombie Point where the Reverend Mr Smith was to meet them. The wind and waves were too strong for the steamer to moor at the jetty and so they were transferred perilously into a small boat in the middle of the Forth. It would have been ironic if in his quest to explore the land of his ancestor Verne should have lost his own life. By hoisting a sail, the boat reached the landing stage and the pair was able to clamber onto dry land. Here, the priest was waiting for them and guided them to an inn near the end of the jetty where a roaring fire helped to dry them out[16]. Once restored, the priest, who spoke excellent French, led the way across sodden fields and after an hour and a half they approached the park of Oakley Castle.

In fact 'Oakley Castle' was Verne's manner of referring to Inzievar House, located approximately a mile south of the village of Oakley. This baronial mansion was newly-built to the design of David Bryce, an Edinburgh master architect of the Scottish 'baronial' genre. It had been built by the brother of the Reverend Mr Smith, Archibald Smith-Sligo, a widower who had recently married Lady Harris, née Margaret Sligo, a wealthy widow. Archibald Smith had previously lived in the Rue Vaugirard in Paris and returned to Scotland after the death of his first wife in 1855. Margaret Sligo's first husband was Sir William Cornwallis Harris. He was a Knight Major in the East India Company and was an accomplished painter, writer and diplomat. After marrying Margaret Sligo in 1845, he returned alone to India where he died of 'lingering fever' near Poona in 1848. Margaret, only 25 at the time, did not see her husband for the last two years of his life. The re-marriage of the two prematurely widowed persons brought together a combination of wealth and cultivated European taste expressed in the décor of Inzievar House which impressed Verne immediately.

The income from the agricultural estate, mineral extraction and the Forth Ironworks at Oakley ensured the degree of wealth necessary to build a handsome mansion fronted by an open terrace with excellent southern views across the Forth valley. Behind the 'castle', stables, green-houses and kitchen gardens were set in mixed woodland copses.

Inzievar House Oakley, Verne's 'Ockley Castle', viewed from across the fields traversed by Verne, Hignard and the Reverend Mr Smith.

A manservant opened the door and ushered the three men into an antechamber where they divested themselves of their saturated cloaks. The priest poured them a large tot of spirits before mounting a staircase and guiding them to a room where dry clothes had been laid out for their convenience. Thus comforted, Verne was able to take in the magnificence of the house. Verne was amazed at the opulence of the drawing room, hung with Italian and Flemish paintings. The Reverend Mr Smith had studied in Italy and his elder brother was also a regular visitor to the Continent. Clearly both were enthusiastic collectors of fine art[17]. The exterior of the mansion was described by Verne as being irregular and this is evident in the present building. The façade shows an asymmetric mix of walls and turrets to which a handsome *orangerie*, considered by the architect Bryce to be one of his greatest achievements, is attached. After admiring the interior, the two friends were offered a gargantuan feast by the priest, but he was then called away to visit a sick parishioner. Bidding his guests farewell, he ordered his baillie to complete the tour of the castle and its grounds. The trio mounted the roof where a platform was equipped with a telescope. From here a panorama dominated the Forth valley to the south and the mining complex around Oakley to the north, including the mine and iron works belonging to the Smith family[18]. The tour continued to the grounds adjacent to the mansion. Here the baillie showed them the stables and greenhouses. The latter, exposed to the south, were groaning with fruit and were so designed as to supply the castle with early fruit and vegetables[19]. Declining the offer to visit the coal mine, the group returned to the house to change back into their clothes and to partake of a farewell whisky before being driven by the baillie to the railway station half a mile away. Verne and his companion were entranced by Inzievar House. On the one hand they were impressed by its modernity, and on the other by the luxury of its interior with fine art, furniture and fittings of the highest quality. Sadly, over the generations,

To the best of this author's knowledge, this is the only original document signed by Verne in the public domain in Scotland. It is a reply to a request for an autograph by a Miss Bryce. Inzievar House was built by David Bryce but this is probably coincidental. The letter demonstrates the illegibility of Verne's handwriting.
University of Glasgow Library, Special Collections

the wealth of the Smith-Sligo family declined and eventually in 1985 the mansion was sold and subsequently sub-divided into flats. Thanks to the kindness of some of the present occupants, this author has been able to visit Inzievar House, see its grounds and admire the view from the tower. It needs little imagination to reconstruct the scenes witnessed by Verne even if the pictures by the grand masters and other features of the décor have disappeared under the auctioneer's hammer.

Onward to the Clyde

Oakley railway station was served by the Stirling and Dunfermline Railway, which transported the two friends to Stirling station. Here, confusion reigned, for after buying tickets to Glasgow they had trouble finding the correct platform since Stirling was served not only by the Stirling and Dunfermline Company, but also by the new Dunblane, Doune and Callander Railway, by the Forth and Clyde Junction Railway and by the Scottish Central Railway. The station had two platforms, one of which was an 'island' platform with tracks on two sides and thus three possible departures for Verne to choose from. After a false start, which almost took them back to Oakley, they boarded the 7.36pm Scottish Central train to Glasgow and in the late evening the train threaded its way through the long tunnel, well known to present day travellers, and arrived at Glasgow's Queen Street Station at 8.55pm. Exiting the station the friends turned left into George Square and entered the first hotel that they saw, Comrie's Royal Hotel[20]. It is unsurprising that they chose the first hotel adjacent to the station since they had been travelling by cab, steamer, on foot and by two trains for approximately fourteen hours. By now, the supper had a familiar ring: cold meat washed down with tea. After this modest repast, they decided to see Glasgow by night and strolled through darkened streets past unlit buildings to reach the Clyde at Glasgow Bridge. Verne remarked that this no longer felt like Scotland and that a resemblance to Liverpool was apparent[21]. In this judgement Verne was both right and wrong. His only point of comparison thus far was Edinburgh, and clearly Glasgow was a very different kind of city. In effect, he was comparing Glasgow with his preconceived image of traditional Scotland, whereas Glasgow was redolent of a very different character –

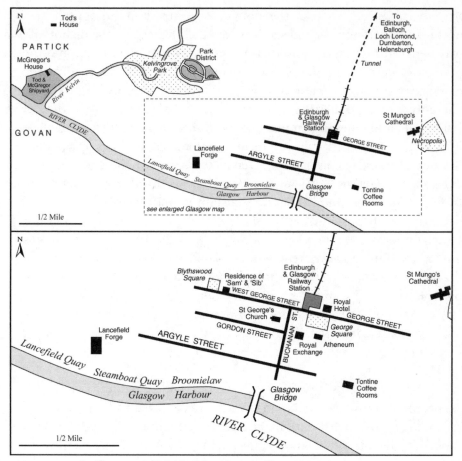

FIG. 6 Jules Verne's Glasgow

the Scotland of entrepreneurs, industry, technical modernisation – energetic and outward-looking [FIG. 6].

Following Argyll and Buchanan Streets, the pair regained their hotel and, after such an exhausting day, decided on an early night. Their plan was to rise early to see more of Glasgow before setting off for their true objective, the lakes and mountains of the Highlands.

Then, as now, Edinburgh and Glasgow could not have been more different from each other in terms of the physical setting, the economy and the society. Whereas Edinburgh had a distinctive skyline with Princes Street Gardens as a sort of *cordon sanitaire* between the Old and New Towns, Glasgow developed on a sloping plain orientated towards the River Clyde. Whereas the dominant contrast in Edinburgh was north-south between the old and new divide, in Glasgow the dichotomy was between the industrialised east and the riverside harbour, and the bourgeois west on the unpolluted hills upwind of the city, echoing the east and west ends of London or Paris. At the time of Verne's visit, Glasgow had a population of over 380,000, more than twice that of Edinburgh, and immigration was adding to this total daily. The growth of Edinburgh represented a development of commerce, business and administration of an indigenous nature, given its status as the nation's capital; the expansion of Glasgow was much more external, attracting a population from the Highlands and Ireland to sustain its industries which in turn depended on its port and access to the Atlantic to import raw materials, especially cotton, and to reach worldwide markets. The medieval nucleus around the Cathedral thus represented a small and declining proportion of the built-up area and Verne spent little more than an hour in this decaying part of the city. By contrast, the fine commercial buildings of Glasgow city centre and the animation of the riverside impressed Verne more although, as at Edinburgh, the statuary he witnessed at George Square left him unmoved, even though the dominant statue was of his literary hero Sir Walter Scott.

Tuesday dawned with a heavy drizzle but, undeterred, the two friends set off for a morning's sightseeing. Verne was amazed to find the streets throbbing with activity, but Hignard reminded him that Glasgow was in rapid expansion and its population had grown fivefold over recent decades. They headed east along George Street on foot between smoke blackened buildings and straddled filthy open streams to reach the Cathedral. To their disappointment the Cathedral was locked and the spectacular necropolis, apart from the connection with Rob Roy's hiding place, was of little interest to him. Frustrated by an unproductive and saturated morning, the friends sought the shelter of a cab and instructed the coachman to take them on a tour of the city centre. At once their spirits rose as they surveyed handsome business and public buildings. It is likely that their route followed the Trongate since Verne was later to initiate the plot of one of his Scottish novels, *The Blockade Runners*, in the Tontine Hotel, a prominent building on the Trongate and unmistakable by virtue of its name emblazoned on the façade.

Arriving at Glasgow Bridge, the coachman followed the quays of the port, probably as far as Partick. Verne admired the frenetic activity and the immense value of cargoes being handled, but still felt that Liverpool held the upper hand as a maritime spectacle, having more the air of a seaport whereas Glasgow was clearly a river port. From the Clyde, the coachman headed north across the Kelvingrove Park into the new bourgeois suburb of the Park area. Verne later failed to find the place on his map, but his description of new mansions laid out in circular form surrounded by parkland leaves no doubt as to the route. Returning to George Square lunch was now pressing, for the most exciting stage of their excursion awaited them in the afternoon. After a repast of cold salmon, the pair strolled to Queen Street station and caught the Edinburgh and Glasgow Railway Company train to Balloch in an open third-class carriage which was totally exposed to the rain[22]. By now, they were well behind the schedule produced by Margaret Bain.

The Highlands at Last!

Gazing through the rain, Verne remarked on Dumbarton Castle with its association with Marie Stuart, but then the train turned north to reach the terminus at Balloch Pier on Loch Lomond. They rushed from the train to gain a good vantage point on the *Prince Albert*, the steamer that was to take them to Inversnaid, towards the northern end of the loch[23]. The steamer headed for Balmaha and then crossed the loch, threading its way through the islands to Luss. In spite of the rain, Verne was determined to miss nothing in the landscape and regaled Hignard with tales of the battles between the MacGregor and Colquhoun clans. Rossdhu House, the headquarters of the Colquhoun clan, was clearly visible on the approach to Luss and was later adopted by Verne as 'Castle Malcolm' in his later novel *The Children of Captain Grant*. At last, Ben Lomond reared its head above the clouds, cascades of water plunged down the mountain side and, as the loch narrowed, the precipitous shores added to the drama of the landscape[24].

> The mountain appeared at last, its feet lapped by the waters of the loch, its head hidden in the clouds. At first Jacques [Verne] found it difficult to accept that it was over a thousand metres high. Soon, however, the peak emerged from the clouds and the

mountain stood revealed in all its 'stern, wild majesty!' Jacques grabbed his friend's arm and exclaimed 'Look at that! You must be able to see half of Scotland from up there'

Backwards to Britain (Chapter 32)

Mooring briefly at Tarbert to allow passengers who were headed westwards towards Loch Fyne and Inverary to disembark, the steamer recrossed the loch to Inversnaid and the two friends disembarked against the background of a roaring waterfall in full spate after the heavy rain. The adjacent inn afforded them the chance to consume a rather rough whisky before mounting the coach service operated by the Earl of Breadalbane[25]. The coach bore the Earl's arms and the coachman wore his livery. The friends mounted the roof of the coach and, looking backwards, marvelled at the panorama of the 'Arrochar Alps'. Verne describes piles of rocks along the road side as 'cairns'. There is no sign of such structures now and they may simply have been piles of boulders cleared when the rough road was built, or may have been erected to mark the path when covered in snow in the long winter. Visibility was

Carriages take passengers from Inversnaid on Loch Lomond to Stronachlachar on Loch Katrine as followed by Verne in 1859. In the background are the 'Arrochar Alps', much admired by Verne.

Stirling County Library and Archives Service

poor in the pouring rain and Verne's imagination may have led him astray. The coach struggled up the steep incline from Loch Lomond and then accelerated past Loch Arklet. Within the hour it descended to the shores of Loch Katrine at Stronachlachar. Alongside a little inn, the ss *Rob Roy* awaited its passengers and Verne and Hignard embarked[26]. Surprisingly, given that shortly afterwards Queen Victoria was to inaugurate the opening of the water supply from Loch Katrine to Glasgow, replacing the pestilential existing supply from the polluted Clyde, Verne makes no mention of this fact, even though the works would have been visible.

As the steamer made its way towards the Trossachs pier, Verne's imagination ran riot. Here he was in the heart of Rob Roy country, the scene of Scott's epic poem *Lady of the Lake*, and a country populated by goblins and fairies in local legend. In the space of roughly the hour that the little steamer took to travel the length of the loch, we must imagine that Verne had decided that here was a setting worthy of a major novel and that the supernatural atmosphere would inspire one of his most endearing characters. The novel would be *The Underground City* and the character Jack Ryan, a firm believer in supernatural events (Chapter 6). Verne's reveries were interrupted by a piper's lament and his musician friend took down the notation with a view to a future composition. Landing at the Trossachs pier, the friends boarded a coach to Callander since their morning's sightseeing in Glasgow meant that they

The Stronachlachar Hotel and the transfer of passengers to and from the steamer *Rob Roy*.
Anonymous postcard, Courtesy Y. Finlayson

Loch Katrine from the summit of Ben Aa. Verne referred to the
Loch and the Trossachs as 'magnificent landscapes whose sublime
beauty defies the imagination'.
Courtesy Y. Finlayson

had to abandon 'Amelia's' schedule, which would have taken them by
coach to Stirling and on by train to Edinburgh that evening. Instead, they
took the coach past the newly-built Trossachs Hotel and, at walking
pace, along the hilly road to Callander. Verne was overwhelmed by the
beauty of the Trossachs and, after climbing beside the coachman

> ... turned one last time to bid goodbye to those magnificent land-
> scapes whose sublime beauty defies the imagination.
>
> *Backwards to Britain* (Chapter 34)

On arriving at Callander, the exhausted travellers swallowed a pint of excellent 'two penny' ale before boarding the train on the newly-opened line to Stirling, reached an hour later[27]. Hunger drove the friends to look for a hotel, and walking from the station up into the town centre they found the Golden Lion Hotel[28]. Sustenance took the habitual form of cold meats and tea after which they fell asleep exhausted from a long but memorable day.

It is interesting to reflect that although Verne had limited funds at his disposal and complained of the cost of accommodation, he and Hignard stayed in relatively expensive hotels in Edinburgh, Glasgow and Stirling. Perhaps as it was his first visit abroad, and being unable to speak English, Verne felt reassured by using hotels with a certain standing. Moreover, at this time the hotel infrastructure was less diversified than today, with a sharp contrast between good hotels at one extreme, and inns, taverns and lodging houses of dubious quality and security at the other. We can also suggest that Verne, although not affluent, was nevertheless from a bourgeois background and would incline to hotels appropriate to this standing.

This first encounter with the Highlands was imprinted on Verne's mind and memory. He was inspired to use the locality of Loch Katrine in his novel *Les Indes noires*, (*The Underground City*), and 20 years later, on his second visit to Scotland, he was to repeat this circuit, albeit in the reverse direction.

Journey's End

The remainder of Verne's first visit to Scotland was a relative anticlimax. He woke up to sunshine, and a morning's sightseeing in the historic and picturesque town beckoned. From their hotel the friends strolled the half mile or so that leads from the Golden Lion Hotel past the cemetery to the castle esplanade. Here Verne's ardent desire to see Highland dress was fulfilled, for the soldiers guarding the castle were wearing full military regalia including pleated kilt and sporran. After admiring the view extending to Ben Lomond to the west and the meandering Forth to the east, they descended to the railway station for the last leg of their Scottish tour. Here a bonus was experienced in the form of a guard of Highland soldiers awaiting the passage of the Royal Train through Stirling en route to Balmoral. Queen Victoria had arrived in Edinburgh

Stirling's 'Golden Lion Hotel' where Verne and Hignard spent their last night
in Scotland in 1859. The facade is virtually unchanged since that time.
Stirling County Library and Archives Service

the previous morning and after descending at St Margaret's station had
been greeted by a crowd of 20,000 cheering citizens according to *The
Scotsman* newspaper. After Verne and Hignard left Stirling aboard the
10.35am Scottish Central train for Edinburgh, the Royal Train rushed
by in the opposite direction[29]. At Stirling station the *Edinburgh Courant*
newspaper reported that the Provost and magistrates of Stirling, together
with many other persons, waved to Queen Victoria and a 21 gun salute
was fired from the castle.

Just over an hour later, after passing through Linlithgow, with Verne
remarking on the birthplace of Marie Stuart, the train plunged through
the tunnel at Haymarket to emerge in Princes Street Gardens, and came
to a halt at Edinburgh's General Railway Station at noon[30]. It was
lunchtime, so the pair revisited their tavern in the High Street for the
now inevitable lunch of cold meats and frothing ale. For reasons of time,
expense and their previous unfortunate experience on the North Sea, the

friends agreed to abandon their initial plan to return to London by steamer in favour of an overnight train. This allowed them a free afternoon for further exploration and, rather than collect their luggage from Inverleith Row immediately, they decided to visit the port of Leith. To their astonishment they discovered a ship flying the *Tricolour* in the harbour. It was a French naval sloop and they did not hesitate to board where they were entertained to conversation, cigars and wine by the second in command. Verne had a lifelong passion for ships and, surprisingly, in view of his dislike of violence, this included warships and their armoury. The *Edinburgh Courant* of 31 August reported that the *Galilée*, a small French war paddle steamer with two large guns, had entered the Victoria Dock. It seems likely that this was the vessel that Verne visited, although a second French boat, the *Corse*, was also in the dock. The encounter with their fellow countrymen appeared to symbolise the fact that their visit to Scotland was nearing its end and the long journey back to France about to begin. Following the shore to Newhaven, they retraced their steps to recover their bags from the charge of servants at William Bain's house, the family being absent. By now there was just time to fortify themselves for an overnight journey with a final meal in the High Street and:

> with heavy hearts, they walked down the Canongate one last time, waved goodbye to Holyroodhouse... An hour later they were back at the station with their luggage and after one last sad glance at Edinburgh Castle Jacques [Verne] followed his friend [into the station].
>
> *Backwards to Britain* (Chapter 36)

It transpired that their train was an excursion train full of excited and rowdy English day trippers, and having booked third-class tickets the pair found themselves on wooden seats in an overcrowded, dank compartment for a miserable 15 hour journey to London[31]. Their magical visit to Scotland thus finished on a note of bathos. Their brief stay in London need not concern us here beyond remarking that Verne witnessed the giant steamship the *Leviathan* under construction in Millwall. Verne was to board this vessel with his brother Paul in Liverpool in 1867 under its new name of *Great Eastern*, to make his only visit to America, taking in New York and the Niagara Falls. As already noted, this voyage was to inspire his novel *Une ville flottante* (*The Floating City*) published in 1869.

In his conclusion to *Backwards to Britain*, Verne admits the superficiality of such a brief visit to Scotland and that his writing must rely on imagination as well as experience:

> They [the two travellers] will have felt Liverpool and formed an impression of Edinburgh; they will have glimpsed Glasgow, guessed at Stirling, groped at London. They will have touched mountains and skimmed over lakes, imagined if not recognized new customs, geographical variations, strange manners, national differences. They will have sensed much – but in truth seen nothing!
>
> Only now, on their return, can their serious exploration begin, for imagination will henceforth be their guide as they travel backwards through their memories.
>
> *Backwards to Britain* (Chapter 48)

This afterthought of Verne's was to prove prescient, for he did indeed apply his creative imagination to writing novels set in Scotland. Moreover, in this chapter we have presented all the evidence required to prove that *Backwards to Britain* is in fact an autobiographical account. All the details of places and persons which can be verified coincide exactly with Verne's description of his visit and strongly suggest that he kept a very detailed diary of his journey, sadly not in existence, at least in the public domain.

One further aspect of Verne at this stage in his life is worthy of comment. Since adolescence and throughout much of his later life, Verne suffered from a variety of illnesses. In particular he suffered from intermittent facial paralysis, chronic digestive disorders that he described in graphic biological detail in correspondence with friends and family, as well as recurrent migraines, bilious attacks, headaches, influenza and a catalogue of minor complaints. The picture of his early years in Paris is one of a young man physically and mentally distressed by illnesses. Ironically, on this 1859 visit to Scotland at the age of 31 there is no mention of these maladies. In the space of only five days in Scotland, he travelled on seven trains, three steamers, six coaches, swam in the freezing North Sea and walked over 30 miles, including the strenuous ascent of Arthur's Seat. In addition, he consumed gargantuan meals at the house of William Bain and at Inzievar House and ate copiously at other times. He had a substantial alcohol intake including many pints of beer and glasses of rum, sherry, port, whisky, claret and sauternes. All this was in a foreign land whose language he could not speak, and for the most part in cold and windy weather, and he kept a series of late nights. For a young man who claimed to be subject to poor health, this was a remarkable accomplishment. It suggests that some of his health problems were induced by the stress of living in Paris, struggling to make a successful career, and supporting a wife and young family in the early years of his marriage. It seems that when he got away from this environment and was exposed to stimulating situations, his health improved. Perhaps, therefore, his health problems were psychosomatic, although it may be that they were the first signs of the diabetes that was to dog his older years and eventually led to his death. Whatever the explanation, he approached his visit to Scotland with gusto and on his return to France commenced writing up his experiences.

The literary legacy

Verne had spent barely a week in Britain and yet the impact on his future literature was to be immense. His account of the journey, written shortly after his return, was later rejected by his eventual publisher, Pierre-Jules Hetzel. Thankfully, the manuscript survived and is now available in its French original and in the English translation as *Backwards to Britain* which has featured throughout this chapter. Without this testament it would have been impossible to explain how his Scottish novels were derived, for it is clear that secondary sources, such as guide books, would not have sufficed to provide the intimate familiarity with local detail that is evident in his books. Verne did not conceal the fact that both published travel accounts and fiction, especially Walter Scott, coloured his imaginative writing, but it is clear that his own experience and notes were crucial when he came to write his 'Scottish' novels or to insert Scottish heroes and heroines in his other works.

If *Backwards to Britain* was his definitive, largely factual response to his first visit to Scotland, Verne was to draw on this 1859 experience as a launch pad for a series of 'Scottish' novels which form the substance of Part Two of this book. They range from a lively novella, *Les Forceurs de Blocus*, (*The Blockade Runners*), 1865, to a global tour de force, *Les enfants du capitaine Grant* (*The Children of Captain Grant*) 1866. This was followed by his most ambitious Scottish novel in a literary sense, *Les Indes noires, (The Underground City)*, 1876. It is almost a *roman noir*, the macabre atmosphere being enhanced by the fact that much of the action takes place underground.

Verne arrived in Edinburgh an unknown and struggling author and librettist. How different his return was to be 20 years later.

Notes

1 This was 'Uncle Prudent', a retired sea captain who lived on a farm in the hamlet of La Guerche some 15 kilometres south west of Nantes, in the commune of Brains of which he was the mayor.

2 The manuscript of the book was rejected by Verne's publisher, Hetzel, but was rediscovered and published posthumously in 1989 as *Voyage à reculons en Angleterre et en Ecosse*, le Cherche Midi, Paris.

3 The English translation of this book was published in 1992 as *Backwards to Britain*, Chambers, Edinburgh, with an introduction and notes by William Butcher.

4 An English translation of this remarkable book, with an extended intro-

duction and annotation, is provided by *The Adventures of Captain Hatteras*, Oxford World's Classics, Oxford University Press, 2005, translated by William Butcher. The construction and operation of the *Great Eastern* is detailed in Dugan, J, *The Great Iron Ship*, Sutton Publishing Ltd, 2003, which includes extensive reference to Verne as a passenger aboard the transatlantic crossing.

5   Verne terms the station as being the terminus of the Caledonian Railway. This confusion arose because the Caledonian had 'through train' status, that is, a number of its carriages would be attached to the London and North Western Railway Company's trains as far as Carlisle. Only after Carlisle, when a Caledonian Railway locomotive in its distinctive sparkling blue paintwork took over these coaches, did the train become a specifically Caledonian express. The 1859 Caledonian Railway timetable for August 1859 confirms the route and timings cited by Verne. *Time Tables of the Caledonian Railway, no 146, August, 1859*. A detailed history of the remarkable Caledonian Railway is provided by Nock, OS, *The Caledonian Railway*, Ian Allan London, 1963, 190pp.

6   Lothian Road Station was a primitive structure built of wood. It was opened in 1848, destroyed by fire in 1890 and rebuilt in 1894, re-baptised as 'Princes Street'. The station closed in 1965 but the grandiose station hotel still remains, mirroring the vast North British Hotel at the opposite end of Prince's Street built in 1902 and now re-named as The Balmoral Hotel.

7   The existence of Lambré's Hotel is confirmed by the *Edinburgh Post Office Directory* for 1859. Their voracious hunger may be explained by the fact that no dining facilities were available on the eight-hour journey from Liverpool.

8   Verne describes the tavern as being 'outside the Tron Church'. According to the 1859 Post Office Directory, there were no taverns close to the Tron Church on the High Street, only coffee houses. However, immediately behind the Tron Church is the tiny Hunter Square, in which number 10, closest to the church, was a tavern belonging to John Spence. Discreetly separate from the Tron Church and the nearby St Giles Cathedral a tavern selling alcohol and meals would have caused no offence, although as Verne was to discover, it would not have been open on a Sunday. This is the most likely tavern where Verne and Hignard dined and where they had supper before taking the train to London. Verne would use the Tron Kirk in a dramatic manner, and incorrectly in terms of religious denomination, in a later novel, *Mirifiques aventures de Maître Antifer*, 1894 (*The Fabulous Adventures of Maître Antifer*). A revealing account of inns and taverns at the

time of Verne's visit is Stuart, Marie S, *Old Edinburgh Taverns*, Robert Hale Ltd, Edinburgh, 1952.

9   The reference to Nodier refers to his guide book *Promenade de Dieppe aux montagnes d'Ecosse*, Barba, Paris, 1821. It has been translated as *Promenade from Dieppe to the mountains of Scotland*, Blackwood, Edinburgh, 1822. Verne made extensive use of this guide book, shared many of Nodier's opinions, especially on architecture, and used parts of Nodier's narrative in his Scottish novels. A further work of Nodier, his novella *Trilby*, published in 1882, was probably known to Verne. It is set in the Trossachs and Argyll and is a tale of fairies and imps. Nodier, C, *Trilby, ou le Lutin d'Argyll*, Daedalus European Classics, Cambridge, 1993.

10   1861 *Census of Population,1861*, Parish of St Bernard, Burgh of Edinburgh, page 7. William Bain left the City of Glasgow Bank well before the crash of that bank to become Joint Cashier, Bank of Scotland, before dying in 1882 at the age of 68, by which time, with his family of five children having left home, the Bains resided in more modest accommodation in Coates Gardens near Haymarket railway station. Bain's will and testament showed that he left an estate of £3,254, a comfortable amount at that time.

11   The family conversion to Catholicism can be traced back to William's father James Smith, born in the Shetlands and a successful lawyer. He had risen to the rank of Solicitor in the Supreme Court in Scotland before marrying a Catholic and converting to her faith. Inevitably, after resigning from his legal career he devoted his life to theological scholarship. He had seven children of whom the oldest was Archibald, the builder and owner of Inzievar House and elder brother of William Smith, the 'Reverend Mr S'. On becoming a widower, Archibald married a certain Margaret Harris Sligo, a wealthy widow, and adopted the surname Smith-Sligo. (*Census of 1861*, Parish of Saline, no 455, Book 6). The family archives have been acquired by The National Library of Scotland, *Acc 1286* and *Acc 8287*. The family heraldic arms are carved into the façade of the mansion and have the motto *Seligo Veritatem*, 'search the truth', in this case the 'true' (ie Catholic) faith. The architectural records of Inzievar House are held in the archives of the Royal Commission on the Ancient and Historical Monuments of Scotland, no. F/5316. An interesting illustrated account of the development of the Catholic church in Oakley, which makes reference to Verne's visit is provided by Nolan, J, *A History of the Holy Name Parish, Oakley*, self published, 29pp.

12   This tattered document, with a translation of Verne's convoluted handwriting

is published in Thompson, IB, 'The visit to Scotland by Jules Verne in 1859', *Scottish Geographical Journal*, vol. 121, no 1, 2005.

13   Verne shows some inconsistency in the naming of steamers. In most cases the names are accurate but are not always allocated to the correct route. In this instance, the *Prince of Wales* is correctly identified on the Stirling route. Navigation as far as Stirling shore was greatly aided by the phenomenon of a double tide, the high tide being prolonged by a second tidal surge above Alloa, the 'Leaky tide', produced by the shallow water depth of the Forth. The introduction of steamers solved the problem of frequent resetting of sails to cope with the changing wind direction caused by the frequent meanders above Alloa.

14   A useful description of the history of steamers on the Forth is provided by Brodie, I, *Steamers of the Forth*, Newton Abbot, 1976

15   The route followed by the *Prince of Wales* is included in Hendrie, W, *Discovering the River Forth*, Edinburgh, 1996.

16   There is now no inn in the tiny hamlet at Crombie Point. However, research identifies that the present 'Black Anchor cottage', built in 1770, was previously the Black Anchor Tavern. From its position close to the end of Crombie Pier we can safely assume that this was the inn patronised by the Reverend Mr Smith and his two guests. The spirit dealer was a John Graham, a widower aged 72.

17   Testament to the high quality of the fine art is provided by *Murray's Handbook for Scotland*, the standard 19th century travel guide. Inzievar House is cited as having landscapes by Aelbert Cuyp, and portraits of Sir Walter Scott by Sir JW Gordon, Mary Queen of Scots by Holbein, St Sebastian by P Veronese and A Doge of Venice by Leonardo da Vinci.

18   The Forth Ironworks opened in 1846 and closed in 1869. With seven blast furnaces it is unsurprising that Verne was impressed by the industrial landscape. The 1861 Census recorded a population of 1,817 in the Oakley Iron Works district, many of whom, including women and children, would have been employed in the works or the nearby coal mines. The 'baillie' who showed Verne round the estate may be identified from the 1861 Census as being Bernard McCann, a 63 year old Irishman who lived in Inzievar with his wife and daughter, and who also served as a game keeper. Consonant with their Catholic faith, the Smith-Sligo family employed numerous Irish domestics.

19   In a county where coal was cheap and plentiful, many wealthy owners of

mansions in West Fife delighted in growing exotic fruit in heated green-houses. Verne remarks on the gas lighting in the house and grounds and exclaims;

> ... all one has to do in this generous land is to dig a hole for perennial heat and light to gush out.

Given that the nearest supply of town gas from Dunfermline at that time was at Cairneyhill, some two miles distant, it seems likely that the estate had its own supply. *Third Statistical Account of Scotland, County of Fife,* Edinburgh, 1952.

20 The 1859 *Post Office Directory* of Glasgow includes the Royal Hotel at 50 George Square. It was a substantial building on the north side of the square but was demolished and replaced by an undistinguished office building in the 1980s. It was commonplace in Scotland at this time for the names of hotels to be preceded by the surname of the proprietor.

21 By this time, approximately a quarter of Glasgow's population was made up of Irish people.

22 The rigorous third-class travelling conditions at this time are graphically described in Martin, D, and Maclean, A, *Edinburgh and Glasgow Railway Guidebook*, Strathkelvin District Libraries, Glasgow, 1992.

23 On this occasion Verne has identified a real vessel on its correct route. The *Prince Albert* was one of a small fleet of paddle steamers named after princes which plied Loch Lomond after the completion of the rail link from Glasgow to Balloch in 1856. Patterson, AJ, *The Victorian Summer of the Clyde Steamers,* Newton Abbot, 1972.

24 Here Verne makes one of his occasional topographical errors. He gives the height of Ben Lomond as being over a thousand metres, whereas in fact it only reaches 973 metres.

25 A large hotel now exists on the site of the inn and alongside the cascade described by Verne. It has its own pier and the view across the loch to the 'Arrochar Alps', much admired by him, is one of the finest on Loch Lomondside.

26 The Stronachlachar Inn was destroyed when the water level of the loch was raised in 1895 to increase Glasgow's water supply and was never rebuilt. The steamship *Rob Roy* was in fact the second ship on Loch Katrine to bear this name, replacing the *Rob Roy I* in 1855. It was jointly owned by the

three hotels at Inversnaid, Stronachlachar and the Trossachs – an early example of integrated tourism. Lloyds, M, *Around Callander and the Trossachs*, Stroud, 1999. The detailed history of each of the *Rob Roy* steamers is given in Duckworth, C, and Langmuir, G, *Clyde River and Other Steamers*, Brown, Son and Ferguson Ltd., Glasgow, Third Edition,1972, p.124–125. Evocative photographs of Stronachlachar and the *Rob Roy* steamers are included in Deayton, A, *Scottish Loch and Canal Steamers*, Tempus, Stroud, 2004, pp.101–103.

27 The 'newly-built' line, the Dunblane, Doune and Callander Railway, was completed in 1858, a year before Verne's visit. It linked Callander with Stirling by joining the Scottish Central line at Dunblane. Thomas, D and Turnock, D, *A Regional History of the Railways of Great Britain*, XV, *The North of Scotland*, Newton Abbot, 1966.

The station used by Verne was a modest affair and was succeeded by a handsome new station built in 'chalet' style some 700 yards to the west, when the Callander and Oban railway opened. The original station served as a goods and mineral depot until 1965. Fryer, C, *The Callander and Oban Railway*, Library of Railway History, Oakwood Press, 1989 and Thomas, D, *The Callander and Oban Railway*, David and Charles, Newton Abbot, 1966, give detailed accounts of this remarkable railway company.

28 The Golden Lion, dating from 1786, in central Stirling, was already a superior hotel at the time of Verne's visit and had been visited both by royalty and appropriately, given Verne's literary aspirations, by Robert Burns. It boasted hot and cold shower baths and an omnibus for the hotel met every train at the station (the precursor of the courtesy bus familiar from airports worldwide today). Carriages were also available for hire; the forerunner of car rentals today. The Golden Lion remains one of the best appointed hotels in Stirling.

29 Marshall, P, *The Scottish Central Railway*, The Oakwood Press, 1998, 250pp.

30 The 'General Station' was the name given to what became Waverley Station. It was 'general' in the sense that in addition to its owner, The North British Railway Company, it was also used by the Scottish Central and the Edinburgh and Glasgow companies. Ellis, H, *British Railway History, 1830–1876*, London, 1954.

31 *The ABC Rail Guide, 1859* shows a departure time of 8.15pm and an arrival in London at 11am, which is very close to Verne's description. The travellers

in Verne's compartment refused to allow a window to be opened which added to his suffering for, as the ABC *Guide* for 1859 points out:

> Fresh air is of greater importance even than the avoidance of draughts and indeed a railway carriage full of passengers, and with all the windows closed, will soon be filled with vitiated air that is insufferable and suggestive only of the Black Hole of Calcutta.

CHAPTER TWO

Return Visit, 1879

IN THE EARLY HOURS of Saturday 12 July 1879, the steam yacht the *St-Michel III* struggled in heavy seas into the port of Leith. Twenty years after his first visit, Jules Verne was once again about to set foot in his beloved Scotland. On his arrival in Edinburgh in 1859, Verne was a struggling author whose literary reputation was largely limited to a *coterie* of theatrical and literary friends in Paris and whose output was voluminous but largely unsuccessful, especially in financial terms. How far his fortunes had changed in 20 years may be gauged from the fact that this time he arrived not in a second class railway compartment, but in his own luxurious steam yacht with a crew of ten. Moreover, the voyage coincided with the recovery of Verne's wife from a life threatening illness and what appeared to be an attempt at a better relationship with his wayward son Michel. We can be sure that this voyage was Verne's response to personal stress – the healing power of putting to sea in his magical boat now that his financial and personal problems had improved. Although now aged 51, he still had over half of his prodigious output before him.

The turning point in Verne's success had been his meeting in 1862 with Pierre-Jules Hetzel, a Parisian publisher. Verne submitted a manuscript to Hetzel which was to appear as *Cinq semaines en ballon, (Five weeks in a balloon)* in 1865. This adventure of a journey in a balloon from Zanzibar across central Africa to the Atlantic coast by a British explorer, Dr Fergusson, was an immediate success and established a genre of adventure writing in which exploration, geography and the use of the latest scientific understanding were key themes. Moreover, a dominant character in the novel was a Scot, Dick Kennedy, the companion of Dr Ferguson on his African adventure. In this first detailed portrayal of a Scot in his novels Verne produces his prototype of the faithful typical Scotsman, which he recycled in his Scottish novels in various capacities. Verne described him as follows:

Dick Kennedy was Scottish in the full sense of the word, open resolute and stubborn. He lived in the small town of Leith, near to Edinburgh, virtually a suburb of 'Auld Reekie'.

(*Five weeks in a balloon*, Chapter 3)

Verne describes him as having been a fisherman, a hunter and skilled marksman. In height and appearance Verne compares him with Halbert Glendinning as portrayed by Scott in *The Monastery*; over six feet tall, possessed of Herculean strength, tanned by outdoor living and with lively dark eyes:

... in fact, something good and solid in his person argued in favour of the Scottish people.

(*Five weeks in a balloon*, Chapter 3)

Under contract to Hetzel, 62 of these *Voyages Extraordinaires* were published, including several which appeared posthumously and in which Verne's own contribution was variable. Whereas some manuscripts had been completed before Verne's death, others were substantially modified by his son Michel and others were written entirely by him and published under his father's name. This collection, skilfully marketed by Hetzel, established a world-wide reputation for Verne, and eventually earned him a comfortable, if not excessively wealthy, existence. In fact, the importance of Pierre-Jules Hetzel in the life of Jules Verne would be worthy of a chapter in itself. Born in Alsace in 1814, Hetzel became a well-known Republican and served as Under-Secretary of State to two ministers. With the *coup d'état* preceding the Second Empire in 1851 Hetzel sought refuge in Belgium until the amnesty proclaimed by Napoleon III in 1859. He became a successful publisher, publishing the works of some of the best known authors of the day, including Balzac and Victor Hugo. He created a magazine intended for children, *Le Magasin d'Education et de Récréation* in 1864, which became the vehicle for Verne to publish his *Voyages Extraordinaires*. The stories appeared as fortnightly instalments which, when complete were bound in a small format book form. Eventually, in a brilliant marketing strategy, they were lavishly illustrated in octavo format and bound within iconic multi-coloured covers which are now collector's items and command high prices. The relationship between Verne and Hetzel was to become both close and turbulent. Hetzel would interfere with Verne's manuscripts, at times exercising a form of censorship, persuading him to change aspects of plots and conclusions, and generally wielding a very heavy editorial hand. Although at times exasperated, Verne held Hetzel in high respect and never turned to an alternative publisher. It is clear that Hetzel benefited considerably financially from Verne's work and initially proposed contracts which were both onerous in terms of output per annum and somewhat miserly in terms of payments given Verne's increasing fame. Nevertheless, the relationship between the two men was extremely close and Verne came to regard him almost as a surrogate father.

From 1865, Verne was in the habit of renting a summer house in Le Crotoy, a small fishing port on the bay of the Somme. By now he was the father of a son, Michel, born in 1861, in addition to being the stepfather of the two stepdaughters from his wife's first marriage. As compared with the noise and bustle of Paris, Le Crotoy afforded him the peace to transform the mountain of notes gleaned from his research in the libraries and learned societies of the capital into exciting novels. Le Crotoy also fulfilled a second passion of Verne's, his love of the sea and sailing. In 1868, on the basis of the royalties from his novels and the proceeds from publishing an encyclopaedic *Geography of France*, he was able to order the construction of a nine metre length yacht of rather basic traditional design, which he named after his son, the *St-Michel*. In fact it was more than just a small boat. He equipped it as a floating library and study where he could escape from the family, and especially the boisterous tantrums of Michel, and concentrate on his writing. It is no coincidence that it was in this boat that one of his most famous books, *Twenty Thousand Leagues under the Sea*, was commenced. Moreover, at full tide the *St-Michel* could set sail and with a local crew Verne was able to indulge in his passion for the sea, making coastwise trips east and west along the French coast, the south coast of England and even as far as London[1]. By now Verne was finding Paris increasingly oppressive and, in 1871, he rented a house in Amiens, his wife's home town. Although visiting Paris regularly for research, to see his publisher Hetzel and also a mistress, Verne now established Amiens as his base and Le Crotoy as his bolthole and access to the sea.

In a series of contracts Verne was required by Hetzel to submit two or three volumes a year and a rapid succession of additions to the *Voyages Extraordinaires* ensued. Best known to English language readers were

Voyage au centre de la terre (*Journey to the centre of the earth*) 1867, *Autour de la lune* (*Around the Moon*) 1872, which encouraged his erroneous reputation as purely a writer in the science fiction genre, and *Le Tour du monde en quatre-vingt jours* (*Around the World in Eighty days*) 1873. But from a Scottish viewpoint, the most significant works were *Les enfants du capitaine Grant* (*The Children of Captain Grant*) 1868, *Les Forceurs de blocus* (*The Blockade Runners*) 1872, *Les Indes noires* (*The Underground City*) 1877 and *Le Rayon vert* (*The Green Ray*) 1882, all of which, apart from *The Green Ray*, drew to a greater or lesser extent on his experiences in Scotland in 1859.

As his fortune increased, in 1876 Verne purchased a handsome sailing yacht which he named the *St-Michel II*[2]. Having too great a draught to moor in Le Crotoy, this boat had Le Tréport on the Picardy coast as its home port. Her fine lines defined the *St-Michel II* as a yacht for cruising and regattas and although Verne enjoyed entertaining his friends and made cruises in the English Channel, it was not the ideal vessel that he longed for. His dream was of an ocean-going boat which could undertake long distance cruises and, in 1877, he found it in the shape of a 27 metre, 67 ton steam yacht awaiting a purchaser in the shipyards of Nantes[3]. On an impulse, which he admitted was an act of folly, Verne

ST. J					YACHT REGISTER.						1881–82
Official Number. Internation'l Code Signal Letters.	Yachts' Names, &c. Beltmakers' Names	Rig. Beltmakers' Names	TONS. Registered Under Deck. Thames Measurement	DIMENSIONS. Registered Dimensions and Thames Measurement Length / Breadth / Depth	Engines of Steamers. Builders of Engines. Materials, Repairs of Vessels, &c., if Classed.	Build. Where. Builders' Names / When.		Owners.	Port belonging to.	Port of Survey.	Character If Assigned, for Hull and Stores. Also Date of Last Survey.
11 M.C.T.J.	St. Joseph	ScwStm Bourster78	— 289	147·6 | 20·7 | 11·1	C.I.2Cy.20"31"-25" 90HP. Jollet&Babin,Nantes	Nantes Jollet&Babin	1878	Marquis de Préaulx	Nantes		
2 28602 Q.B.M.S.	St. Lawrence	Yawl C.Ratsey	41 79	71·2 | 16·5 | 8·9	....	Cowes M.E.Ratsey	1860 5mo.	G. R. Stephenson	Cowes		
3 M.C.F.G.	St. Michel Iron	ScwStm	— 67	107·3 | |	C.2Cy. Jollet&Babin,Nantes	Nantes Jollet&Babin	1876	Jules Verne	Nantes		
4	St. Pierre	Cutter	— 13	34·7 | 10·1 | 7·5	....	Hâvre A.LeMarchnd	1879	Comte H. de Cussy	Ousetrehm		
5 12167 K.W.Q.C.	St. Ursula	Schoonr Lapthorn	150 199	103·9 | 21·3 | 11·1 len.66alt.73	....	Lymingt'n G.Inman	1853	Col. E. H. Kennard, M.P.	London		
6	Salacia	Cutter	— 10	... | ... | ...	....	Jersey Clark	1871	S. B. C. Barrett	Prtsmouth		
7 81629	Salamander	ScwSch	48 63	85·3 | 12·8 | 7·1	C.3Cy.4½",10½"&14½" —9"8HP.Prkns'sPatnt Gr'nwood&Batley,Leeds	London Forrestt&Son	1879	Frederick Power	London		
8	Salamandre	Yawl	— 9	33·0 | 8·2 | 3·9	....	Hâvre A.LeMarchnd	1880	A.Milon	Havre		
9 63357 K.F.M.D.	Sally (late Agnes)	Cutter Lapthrn81	17 28	46·6 | 12·3 | 7·6	....	Beaumaris Owen	1870	Thomas Aveling	Rochester		
20	Salmo	Cutter Lapthrn80	— 6	26·5 | 8·0 | 5·3	....	Barrow Ashburner	1880 5mo.	John Fell	Barrow		

The entry of Verne's Steam Yacht, the *St-Michel III*, in *Lloyd's Yacht Register*.
Courtesy Lloyd's Yacht Register, London

purchased the *St-Michel III* for 55,000 francs. Fitted out with living and writing quarters and with a crew of ten sailors under the command of an experienced master, usually Captain Charles Ollive, Verne was now equipped to voyage at will throughout Northern Europe and the Mediterranean. After a successful proving voyage to Lisbon, Gibraltar, Tangiers and Algiers in 1878, Verne could now turn to northern seas and in July 1879 began his second journey to Scotland, this time literally under his own steam. Commanded by Captain Ollive, the *St-Michel III* left Nantes on Saturday 28 June and sailed in poor weather only reaching Boulogne on the following Tuesday morning, where Verne and his son Michel joined the company, having arrived by train from Amiens. The poor weather persisted and it was not until the following Sunday that the *St-Michel* could put to sea *en route* to England, but above all Scotland. Yarmouth was reached on Tuesday 8 July and while his yacht was coaling, Verne explored Yarmouth and Gorlestone. In fact the stormy weather continued and the *St-Michel* could not set sail northwards until the early morning of Saturday 12 July. The local paper, quaintly-named *The Yarmouth Gazette and North Norfolk Constitutionalist*, confirmed that:

> The elements of late have been more ungenial [sic] than ever, and at present there seems reason to fear that we merge into another dreary winter... umbrellas, waterproofs, macintoshes, and other articles of protection are in general use... the beach is comparatively deserted and wears the appearance more of November than July.

At last, after battling the wind and rain, Verne's yacht entered the port of Leith, not without extreme difficulty, in the early morning of Sunday 13 July[4]. After this stormy passage from Yarmouth, Verne contented himself with a stroll along Princes Street in pouring rain. The rain continued to fall all day Monday and he remained on board the *St-Michel*, working and writing letters. *The Scotsman* newspaper reported on 15 July that:

> ... a strong gusty wind continued to blow from the north east accompanied with drenching showers. According to observations taken from the southern suburbs, the rainfall from nine am Saturday to four o'clock yesterday morning (Monday) was 2.95 inches. Floods on the Water of Leith, which flowed into Leith Harbour, were the highest for 20 to 30 years.

The record of Verne's arrival at Leith in the port register under the command of Captain Charles Ollive.

Courtesy National Archives of Scotland

His close friend, Louis-Jules Hetzel, the son of his publisher, arrived from France by train and joined the group aboard the *St-Michel* which included in addition to Verne, his son Michel and nephew Gaston, a friend of Michel named Sourien[5], and Godefroy, a friend of Jules Verne who frequently accompanied him on his voyages. Tuesday witnessed some improvement in the weather and Verne seized the opportunity to revisit his favourite haunts from 1859. By now the city had attained a population of over 200,000 but Verne had no difficulty in orientating himself. Once more he descended the High Street and Canongate to Holyrood Palace and, in spite of his more than 50 years, scrambled up to the Salisbury Crags. He returned to the *St-Michel* via the castle and Calton Hill. In the evening, Verne took a gentle stroll and visited the French Consul, Monsieur Decourt. There is no evidence to suggest that he tried to revisit the Bain family in Inverleith Row. By the time of Verne's visit, Amelia would have married and her brothers had embarked on business careers, like their father, in banking. No longer required to house a large family, Bain had moved to a more modest house in Coates Gardens, a less fashionable area near Haymarket Railway Station, where both William and his wife Catherine lived for the rest of their lives[6]. Similarly, there is no evidence that Verne revisited Inzievar House. By this time William Smith, who had befriended Verne and Hignard in 1859, had reached the age of 60. He had ascended the Catholic hierarchy and had attained the position of Archbishop of St Andrews and Edinburgh.

Back to the Highlands

By Wednesday 16 July, Verne was ready to leave his beloved boat to set off on an itinerary that was to terminate at the place in Scotland which most enchanted him – the island of Staffa and Fingal's Cave. However, before setting off on this odyssey he was determined to revisit The Trossachs and Loch Lomond, immortalised just two years earlier in his book *Les Indes noires*, (*The Underground City*).

Whereas no direct documentary evidence remains of Verne's 1859 journey other than the single page fragment of his itinerary reproduced in the previous chapter, we can be much more precise as to the 1879 journey thanks to the remarkable survival of the diary of the various voyages that he undertook in his two vessels, the *St-Michel* II and III.

These *carnets de voyages* consist of a simple exercise book bound in a dark cover, with a page size of 11 centimetres in width and 17 centimetres in height. Just over 60 pages of closely written entries in pencil summarise all the sailings made by Verne in these two yachts. The style is very 'telegraphic' and the handwriting difficult to decipher, but it is possible to follow his travels in Scotland exactly and reference to contemporary timetables, travel descriptions and newspapers allows us to fill in the details of his itinerary. Without the existence of these *carnets* it would be impossible to reconstruct the detail of this second journey. The only surviving document in Scotland is the arrival and departure of the *St-Michel* in the Port of Leith records. For copyright reasons, it is not possible to quote the diary entries verbatim, or to reproduce an image of the diaries, which are held in the Central Library of Amiens (MS 101440095. *St Michel*). It is clear from the diary entries that his next Scottish novel, *Le Rayon vert*, (*The Green Ray*) was based exactly on his itinerary from Glasgow to the Hebrides. This correspondence is so close that Verne's 1879 journey can be followed by the map of *The Green Ray* included here in Chapter Seven.

The journey west commenced by early morning train on 16 July from Waverley Station to Callander. From here the group took a coach

The *Prince of Wales* steamer leaves Luss Pier for Balloch with Ben Lomond in the background. This was the route followed by Verne and his companions in 1879.
Mitchell Library, Glasgow

in the reverse direction of his 1859 journey, to the Trossachs Pier. As tourist activity expanded, so the need for horse-drawn carriages increased and the hotels required substantial stabling. At the height of pre-motorised tourism, the Trossachs Hotel had stabling for over one hundred horses and the Inversnaid Hotel sixty. Once more Verne sailed the length of Loch Katrine on the *Rob Roy* steamer to Stronachlachar and onward by coach to Inversnaid, where he revisited the cascade he had admired 20 years earlier and which is still a prominent landmark, especially after heavy rain. From here he boarded the steamer to sail the length of Loch Lomond to Balloch. His diary records the passage via Luss, and he explicitly cites this as being the location of 'Castle Malcolm', the stately home of Lord Glenarvan, the hero of *The Children of Captain Grant*. At Balloch, a connecting train transported the group to Glasgow. A creature of habit, Verne looked no further than the Royal Hotel on George Square to dine and have an early night in anticipation of a long and exciting journey on the morrow[7].

Aboard the RMS *Columba*

Verne rose very early on the morning of Thursday 17 July and made his way with his companions to the Broomielaw Quay. Thus far, he had revisited his favourite haunts of the summer of 1859, but now he was to embark on the exploration of new territory and moreover by his favourite form of transport, by boat! The Broomielaw was heaving with humanity for it was 'Glasgow Fair', the traditional summer holiday, especially enjoyed by the working classes. Moreover, the weather promised to be good for the voyage as the *Glasgow Evening Times* of 17 July stated;

> So far the holiday-makers have had no reason to complain of the weather. Yesterday and the day before, though a little dull, were pleasant enough for holiday purposes and this morning there is promised a warm sunshiny day. There has been in consequence a great overflow of the city population and the steamers and trains to the coast have been well filled.

They made their way through the hurly burly of the crowds on the quay-side boarding the numerous steamers whose sailing schedules almost filled the front page of the day's *Glasgow Herald*. Verne boarded the

Royal Mail Steamer (RMS) *Columba*, pride of the steamer fleet of David MacBrayne and Company[8]. She was newly-built of steel and at 300 feet, the longest of the Clyde steamers as well as being the most rapid and the most lavishly appointed. In addition to a post office aboard and an abundant supply of stationery, she had a fruit stall, newsagent and even a barber. Hot salt baths were available for the revival of passengers who had travelled overnight by train. Old postcards bearing the franked stamp of the *Columba* are now collector's items. She could transport 2,190 passengers and crew and the luxurious dining room could accommodate 130 diners at a time serving breakfast, dinner and afternoon tea for cabin and First Class passengers, enhanced by a selection of spirits and fine wines. Steerage and Third Class passengers had dining facilities in the forecabin. She was a 'swift steamer', capable of 19 knots, and in the busy summer season sailed the first leg of the 'Royal Route' from Glasgow to Ardrishaig. In winter she was laid up in Bowling Basin, the Clyde terminus of the Forth and Clyde canal, and the passenger and mail service was taken over by the equally impressive *Iona*[9]. The Royal Route, which led from Glasgow to Oban, Fort William and via the Caledonian Canal to Inverness, was so called after the itinerary followed by Queen Victoria

The *Columba* with a full head of steam on the Clyde and with a packed passenger load.
McLean Museum and Art Gallery. Inverclyde Council

in 1847 to gain her castle at Balmoral[10]. It was the spine of David MacBrayne's Clyde and West Coast steamer system, in which stops were made at various piers to embark and disembark passengers and mail, and to connect with feeder steamer and rail services.

Promptly at 7am, Captain M'Gaw,[11] the redoubtable master, gave the order to cast off and the *Columba* set sail. Captain M'Gaw was a remarkable sailor who encapsulated the kind of Scottish seaman that Verne admired – strong, calm, skilful, experienced in seamanship across the globe and, underneath a stern exterior, possessing a human and sentimental side. As the *Columba* made frequent moorings to embark and disembark passengers, M'Gaw would have been fully occupied navigating his massive steamer through the dense holiday traffic and negotiating the narrow sea passage through the Kyles of Bute. Given Verne's inability to speak English and with the captain being fully occupied, it is likely that Verne would only have observed M'Gaw without actually meeting him. Verne would almost certainly be ensconced in the saloon rather than being jostled on the crowded open deck. The saloon had two further advantages. Extending to the full width of the steamer, the first Clyde steamer to have this feature, an uninterrupted view of both shores and to the rear of the steamer was available. Moreover, this visibility was also available in the restaurant, which served a breakfast and a cooked dinner en route at midday. A hot breakfast was served immediately on sailing, a facility advertised as allowing passengers an extra hour in bed, an advantage not applicable to the early riser Verne.

After setting sail, the *Columba* proceeded at reduced power on her paddles so as not to jostle other steamers with her wake. Glasgow Harbour extended for two and a half miles downstream from Glasgow Bridge and this slow speed afforded Verne a vantage point from which to observe the activity of the port. She passed the quays, shipyards and industries between the Broomielaw and the twin settlements of Govan and Partick on either side of the Clyde. The *Columba* made her first stop at Partick at 7.15am at the wharf at the mouth of the River Kelvin, the site of Tod and McGregor's shipyard, which Verne had already used as the starting point of his novella *The Blockade Runners*. The next stop was at Greenock where the Custom House Quay was reached at 9am, splendid views of Dumbarton and Helensburgh having been enjoyed en route. Verne would have had clear views of the magnificent villas on the seafront at Helensburgh and the mouth of the Gareloch which he used as the location of the 'cottage' of the Melvill brothers in his next book, *The Green Ray*. After a rapid stop lasting but a few minutes, sufficient time for the boat to be joined by passengers who had arrived by the London and North Western and Caledonian railways, the *Columba* made a second stop at Greenock's Prince's Pier. Here, the steamer connected with trains from the Midland and the Glasgow and South Western rail systems. After a further stop at Kirn, near the mouth of the Holy Loch, the *Columba* reached Dunoon at 9.25am. As the first stop at a holiday resort on the Firth of Clyde, many passengers would have disembarked here. Others, ferried across the Clyde from Craigendoran Pier near Helensburgh, where they would have arrived by train along the north bank, joined the *Columba*.

This connection with train routes at Glasgow, Helensburgh and Greenock, and the subsequent numerous stops in the Firth of Clyde in part explain the success of the *Columba* and its luxurious appointment and quality cuisine. The route and timetable allowed wealthy people, resident in England but with estates in the Highlands, to travel by rail and steamer in the style and comfort to which they were accustomed.

After a brief stop at the pier at Innellan, the *Columba* headed south to its next important destination, Rothesay on the Isle of Bute, reached at 9.50am. Here, the scene at Dunoon would have been repeated as holiday-makers disembarked and others boarded ship. We must imagine that Verne was making notes throughout this journey and it is virtually certain that he was following the route carefully in a French guide book.

After leaving Rothesay, Verne and his friends marvelled at the most spectacular part of the Clyde section of their journey. The *Columba* threaded her way through the fjord of the Kyles of Bute, seemingly with scarcely enough room to pass between the shores. Having rounded the narrows, the steamer again headed south with views of Goat Fell on Arran in the far distance. As Verne and his companions finished their lunch, the *Columba* entered Loch Fyne and sailed northwards on the last leg of her route. Pausing briefly at the pretty little fishing port of Tarbert, she eventually reached the terminus of her service at Ardrishaig at 12.40pm. Here a crowd of passengers was waiting on the pier, which had been lengthened to accommodate the *Columba* and her sister ship the *Iona*, to embark on the return voyage to Glasgow. Meanwhile, the

The *Columba* moored at Ardrishaig on Loch Fyne where Verne transferred
to the canal steamer *Linnet*.
George Washington Wilson Collection, University of Aberdeen

new arrivals disembarked and walked the short distance across the road
to the Crinan Canal where the next boat, the ss *Linnet*, awaited them.
Verne must have been amused and astonished by what was one of the most
bizarre vessels which has ever sailed on Scotland's inland waterways[12]. The
Linnet, introduced to the canal in 1866, could accommodate 200 passengers in its saloon and open deck and had almost the appearance of a
floating bandstand surmounted by a tall chimney stack funnel. She made a
stately passage through the nine locks of the canal to reach the Crinan
Basin in the space of the two hours needed to cover the nine miles linking
Ardrishaig with the open Atlantic. She set off promptly at 1pm and, as was
customary when passing through the staircase of locks at Cairnbaan,
which took 45 minutes to transit, many of the passengers would stroll
along the towpath, often, like Verne, buying a drink of milk from the
urchins who followed the *Linnet's* gentle progress. In fact, because of the
holiday crowds, a second boat, the horse-drawn 'track' boat *Sunbeam*,
followed the *Linnet* [13]. Eventually, moored in Crinan Basin, the passengers disembarked and joined the waiting ps *Chevalier*, commanded by

Captain D McCallum, deputising for the regular captain Captain Campbell who was ill, which was to take Verne and his party on the final leg to Oban. Although at 334 gross tons the *Chevalier* was little more than half the size of the *Columba,* she was a handsome and popular vessel capable of 16 knots and kept in impeccable condition by her crew. The bell sounded for dinner immediately after setting sail and her route to Oban took Verne to the east of Jura and Scarba before threading her way through the archipelago of Seil, Luing and Kerrera to reach Oban Bay. The holiday atmosphere was enhanced by the playing of a German band, the Red Caps! This was a common feature of summer sailings and many of the musicians were German students earning some money by passing among the passengers collecting coins in a scallop shell.

Verne would have seen and heard the mighty Corryvreckan maelström between Jura and Scarba which was to play a crucial role in the plot of *The Green Ray.* Although Verne never visited Seil Island, the *Chevalier* would have passed sufficiently close for Verne to select it also for one of the more farcical episodes in this novel. Finally, mooring at Oban's North Pier, by 6pm Verne was soon comfortably installed in the Caledonian Hotel on Oban's seafront[14].

The Crinan Basin with the *Linnet* in the foreground and the *Chevalier* ready to set sail for Oban.

Courtesy Guthrie Hutton and Stenlake Publishing Limited

The Caledonian Hotel had been completed in 1832 and its proud new owner inserted a prominent advert in *The Scotsman* on 30 June, 1875, addressed:

To Tourists, New "Caledonian Hotel" Oban, Argyleshire.
Duncan McArthur, late of the King's Arms, Port-Glasgow, begs respectfully to intimate, that he has opened the above extensive establishment for Travellers, – the want of which has hitherto been a subject of general complaint by strangers visiting this place... A choice assortment of Foreign Wines and Spirits. Excellent Stabling and Carriages, Cars, Gigs and Saddle Horses, etc lent out to hire.

It had been an exhilarating day and one which must have filled Verne's head with experiences and impressions ready to be translated into novel form. It had been a strange mixture of ever more spectacular scenery, three contrasted steamers, an animated crowd aboard and probably the best weather that he had as yet encountered on either of his Scottish visits. Verne dined in the hotel and had difficulty changing money for the town's banks would have been closed by the time of his arrival. At the time of Verne's visit, Oban had a population of approximately 4,000

The seafront at Oban with the 'Caledonian Hotel' identified by its dome in the centre. Verne walked the short distance to the North Pier, to embark on the *Pioneer* for his journey to Iona and Staffa.
Anonymous postcard, Courtesy R. McCulloch

inhabitants of whom half used Gaelic as their first language. This relatively small population size belied the importance of Oban as a fishing and ferry port, a commercial and market centre and an already expanding tourist centre. Tourism had been stimulated by the accounts of Samuel Johnson and James Boswell of their journey to the Hebrides and even more by the legends of Ossian, by Sir Walter Scott's popular poem *Lord of the Isles* and the report of the visit to Fingal's Cave by Sir Joseph Banks in 1772[15]. *Slater's Street Directory* for 1868 listed 16 hotels of which the grandest were on the northern seafront promenade. The town had five branch banks, well over 30 shops and no less than eight churches. The town was on the cusp of the take off stage of tourist development in the summer months and Verne's exploitation of Oban in this context in *The Green Ray* is entirely credible.

Journey to the Isles

In an interview by Gordon Jones with Verne at his home in Amiens shortly before his death, the author stated:

> I had the most pleasant tour of Scotland, and among other excursions paid a visit to Fingal's Cave in the Isle of Staffa. This vast cavern, with its mysterious shadows, dark, weed-covered chambers, and marvellous basaltic pillars, produced upon me a most striking impression, and was the origin of my book *The Green Ray*[16].

Even before his visit to Staffa, Verne was clearly aware of its significance and had mentioned the island in three of his novels, *Journey to the Centre of the Earth* (1864), *The Mysterious Island* (1875) and *The Chancellor* (1875). In this last book Verne, referring to a small cave, writes:

> M. Letourneur and André who have visited the Hebrides, pronounced it to be a Fingal's Cave in miniature; a Gothic chapel that might form a fit vestibule for the cathedral cave of Staffa.
> *The Chancellor* (Chapter 18)

Friday 18 July was, therefore, one of the most significant days in his creative life and remained as a powerful memory until the end. The day began early at 6am but this was no hardship for Verne, a very early riser who habitually wrote for five hours before lunch. At 8 o'clock, Verne and his companions were summoned aboard the PS *Pioneer* by the ship's bell and set sail from Oban's North Pier[17]. She alternated her route daily, first clockwise then anti-clockwise round the island of Mull. On this day, just as in *The Green Ray*, the route rounded the south of the island with sightseeing stops scheduled at Iona and Staffa before returning to Oban via the Sound of Mull. Rarely, if ever, in Verne's prodigious output can an entire book have been so inspired by a single day's excursion. Moreover, the fact that passengers were able to disembark at Iona and Staffa meant that he was able to make a reconnaissance of the two islands and thus introduce authentic topographical detail into the ensuing novel.

The *Pioneer* sailed out of Oban Bay, via the Sound of Kerrera and headed for the Ross of Mull, the precipitous headlands on the south west coast of the island. En route magnificent views of Mull's highest peak, Ben More[18], and on the mainland to the north the mountains of Lorne capped by Ben Nevis, came into view. After passing the Ross, the *Pioneer* skirted the reefs and islets at the tip of Mull and turned north into Iona Sound and moored close to the island's pier at 11.30am. Here most passengers disembarked, transported the short distance to the shore by rowing boats manned by the island's crofters, who thus gained a supplement to their

Passengers transported by crofters' fishing boat from Iona's landing stage to re-embark on the steamer.

George Washington Wilson Collection, University of Aberdeen

meagre farm earnings. One and a half hours of freetime in the schedule allowed them to explore the island and especially the cathedral site[19].

At this stage, Verne's own experience diverged from *The Green Ray*. For reasons of the plot, the *dramatis personae* of the novel remain on Iona for almost a week. Nevertheless, Verne explored the ruins of the cathedral site and an entire chapter of the novel is set amongst them. In turn, Verne investigated St Oran's chapel, the cemetery with the tombs of over 50 kings, including two Norwegians and one French, and finally the cathedral ruins. Even McLean's Cross finds its place in the novel. It is highly probable, as was the custom at that time, that Verne's group was escorted by a guide. The group of Frenchmen made their way back to the pier to continue their voyage and at 12.15pm the *Pioneer* set sail for the half hour cruise to Staffa.

If the view from the summit of Arthur's Seat was the highlight of Verne's 1859 visit, there is no doubt that Staffa was the peak experience of his return to Scotland 20 years later. Favoured by good weather and a calm sea, he was able to join the other passengers in the lifeboat manned by sailors from the tiny island of Gomera who habitually met the *Pioneer*. Verne was thus able to penetrate the interior of Fingal's Cave, to admire the basalt pillars, to marvel at the cathedral-like vault of the interior and to hear the 'music' of the waves against the walls of the cave.

The impression left on Verne was overpowering and he later put his own thoughts into the mouth of the heroine of *The Green Ray*, Helena Campbell:

What an enchanted place this Fingal's Cave is! Who could be so dull of soul as not to believe that it was created by a god for sylphs and water nymphs! And for whom do the wandering winds strike music from this vast Aeolian harp? Surely this was the unearthly music that Waverley heard in his dreams?

The Green Ray (Chapter 19)

Verne was able to explore the tiny island, seeing the other caves, and the landing place at Clamshell Bay. From the summit he became aware that this would be the ideal location to see the 'green ray' appear fleetingly at sunset on the marine horizon, which was to become the climax of his future novel. Having made the most of the hour and a half visit to

Verne visited Staffa in 1879 on a day as calm as this view.
Fingal's Cave is shown on the right.
Courtesy Y. Finlayson

Staffa, Verne rejoined the *Pioneer* for the last stage of the excursion. The steamer headed for the northern tip of Mull and entered the narrow and sheltered Sound of Mull and headed south for Oban. A perfect summer evening allowed the *Pioneer* to steam serenely, and on his return in the *St-Michel* to France Verne wrote to his friend Louis-Jules Hetzel, the son of his publisher, that the journey from Dover to Le Havre had been so calm that 'One would have believed that we were on the Sound of Mull!'

The *Pioneer* moored at Oban at 6pm and the group returned across the road to the Caledonian Hotel for a last night ashore in Scotland.

It was time to return to Edinburgh and rejoin the *St-Michel*, and the quickest way was to take the train. However, the Callander to Oban Railway did not reach Oban until the following year and so at 9.30 in the morning of 19 July, the group took the open mail coach linking Oban with the railhead at Dalmally, 26 miles and over an hour and a half away. North of Oban the road follows the coast of Loch Linnhe and then Loch Etive. Between these two sea lochs lie the Falls of Lora where a submarine rock outcrop causes rapids, in effect a sea waterfall. On the rising tide, and particularly on the ebb tide, dramatic whirlpools are produced. Verne would have passed within a few metres of this marine disturbance and it would have reminded him of the Corryvrechan maelström. He rejoiced in the spectacular scenery of the Pass of Brander before joining the train which took them to Stirling. Changing at Stirling to the Caledonian train for Edinburgh, Verne reached his destination at 6.30pm and boarded his beloved *St-Michel* at Leith.

So ended Jules Verne's second visit to Scotland. In some ways it was more successful than the first. He had a little more time and more money, was less excitable and covered more territory whilst also revisiting his favourite haunts from 1859. Moreover, the sights, sounds and itinerary were to provide him with the material for his penultimate Scottish novel, *The Green Ray*, which was unique in its genre in the whole of the *Voyages Extraordinaires*; a light-hearted romance in which the best-drawn character is a heroine, Helena Campbell.

His departure from Scotland was not to be any easier than his arrival. No sooner had he embarked on the *St-Michel* than the weather deteriorated again. Leaving on the early morning high tide on Sunday 20 July, the gale forced the *St-Michel* to ride out the storm overnight in the Firth of Forth. Monday saw Verne seek shelter in the harbour at Leith before once more setting sail in the early morning. Again, the weather defeated the *St-Michel* and she anchored in the lee of the south shore of the Firth. The atrocious weather which had dogged both the arrival and the departure of the *St-Michel* recall the comment by Stevenson in his essay *Edinburgh Picturesque Notes*, that:

> Edinburgh pays cruelly for her high seat in one of the vilest climates under heaven. She is liable to be beaten by all the winds that blow, to be drenched with rain, to be buried in cold sea fogs... The weather is raw and boisterous in winter, shifty and ungenial in summer.

Finally, on 23 July, the weather improved and Verne sailed in calm conditions, reaching Yarmouth once more the following day. They paused only off Prestonpans to land Louis-Jules Hetzel by ship's boat to return to Paris by train. In a letter to Verne dated 31 July 1879, his publisher Jules Hetzel reports that his son had thoroughly enjoyed his trip and stated that 'Scotland is an unforgettable country'. Moreover he had enjoyed the company of the group and especially of Michel. This suggests that Verne's hope of a happy and healing voyage may well have been fulfilled. This time, Verne had no need to take shelter, for the excellent weather held. After anchoring overnight at Dover, the *St-Michel* finally reached Le Havre on Saturday 26 July.

Journey's End

On 23 July Jules Verne had left Scotland for the last time. In total his two Scottish journeys had lasted only 12 days ashore and yet this inspired five novels set entirely or partly in Scotland. Ironically, his second, and arguably his most fulfilling visit, led only to one of them, albeit a significant novel, *The Green Ray*. In fact, the publication of this final Scottish novel coincided with a wider change in orientation in Verne's work away from Britain and towards North America and the Mediterranean. Scotland was to reappear briefly in a further novel, *Mirifiques aventures de Maître Antifer* (*The Fabulous Adventures of Master Antifer*), published in 1894, but apart from this, his attachment to the country, and Britain as a whole, seemed to dwindle. It is as though his admiration for British industrial inventiveness, entrepreneurial dominance and overseas supremacy was waning in favour of the new energy of the United States. The romantic attachment to Scotland seems never to have faded, but he had a prescient feeling that the future of science and technology lay in American hands. In April 1898 he replied to a letter from an American in Pennsylvania[20].

> I hasten to reply to your letter and why should I hesitate to do so since it is from the hand of one of my unknown American friends. Last year I dedicated to them my novel *Le Sphinx des Glaces*[21], and in honour of their great poet Edgar Poe, to demonstrate my gratitude. Next year it will be the whole of the United States which will act as the theatre of my new novel[22]. I hope when you read it that it will give you some pleasure. 25 or 27 years ago, I was able to visit a part of your beautiful country and have kept precious memories[23].

This letter illustrates his affection for the United States, for Verne seldom replied to 'fan mail' at such length and with so much enthusiasm.

Verne's first visit to Scotland in 1859 was that of an excited young man, full of humour, with an eye for the comic as well as enthusiasm for 'his' Scotland. By the time of his second visit, he was established as an author world-wide and was earning his living entirely by his pen. We thus close this first part of this book and turn from a factual account of Jules Verne's travels in Scotland to the fiction that this inspired[24].

Notes

1 The most comprehensive account of the various sailings by Verne in his three boats, and Verne's relationship to the sea in general is, Valetoux, P, *Jules Verne en mer et contre tous*, Magellan, Paris, 2005, 176 pp.

2 Verne insured the *St-Michel II* and the *St-Michel III* with Lloyds of London. Details of the two vessels can be found in *Lloyd's Yacht Register*.

3 Verne purchased the *St-Michel III* from the Marquis de Preaulx. *Lloyd's Yacht Register* shows the marquis as owning several yachts registered at Nantes as home port where he seems to have been something of a dealer in used yachts.

4 The register of shipping for the Port of Leith is a double paged handwritten document. The entry for the *St-Michel III* on 13 July indicates that it is a 'pleasure yacht', captained by C Ollive, arrived in ballast (ie without cargo) from Yarmouth. The re-entry of the storm-bound *St-Michel* on 21 July and departure on 22 July has been added to the original record. As a purely passenger vessel, Verne did not have to pay port dues and so a second separate record was apparently not necessary. National Archives of Scotland catalogue number GD229/2/48 Port Registers, (Leith), 16 May 1879–15 May 1880.

5 The presence of Michel Verne's friend Sourien is stated in correspondence between Jules Verne and Louis-Jules Hetzel. On the evidence of correspondence it seems likely that all of Verne's passengers accompanied him ashore on his Scottish excursion, leaving Captain Ollive in charge of the *St-Michel* in Leith. Verne's nephew Gaston was later to play a catastrophic role in his life, as will be seen later. Dumas, O, Gondolo della Riva, P, and Dehs, V, *Correspondance inédite entre Jules Verne and Pierre-Jules Hetzel, Tome 3*, 2002.

6   Entry in *Confirmations and Inventories*, Edinburgh, 1883.

7   By now, the ownership of the Royal Hotel had passed to James Carrick. In 1879 it had become a prominent hotel occupying much of the north side of George Square.

8   Ownership of many of the shipping services on the West Coast passed from the Hutcheson brothers to David MacBrayne in the late 1870s. David MacBrayne published an annual guide to his company's services entitled *Summer Tours in Scotland*, including a very detailed timetable and descriptive guide to *The Royal Route*. This guide was invaluable in reconstructing the detail and timings of Verne's 1879 voyage to Oban aboard the *Columba*.

9   For a highly illustrated and detailed account of steamer activity on the Clyde in its heyday, including information on the *Columba* see Patterson, AJS, *The Victorian Summer of the Clyde Steamers, 1864–1888*, John Donald, Edinburgh, 2001, 260pp. An excellent pictorial account is provided by McCrorie, I, *Clyde Pleasure Steamers. An Illustrated History*, undated, 96pp. An interesting illustrated account of each of the individual piers is Monteith, J and McCrorie, I, *Clyde Piers a pictorial record*, Inverclyde District Libraries, 1982.

10   Duff, D, *Queen Victoria's Highland Journals*, Lomond Books, 1994, pp 49–56.

11   For a portrait and character sketch of Captain M'Gaw see *The Bailie*, No. 247, 11 July, 1877, Glasgow. This describes M'Gaw as 'cool, watchful and collected. He doesn't mix with his passengers. When off duty he is a genial, pleasant gentleman; but on the bridge of his vessel, he is somewhat of a stern seaman, looking carefully after the lives and limbs of the people who have been entrusted to his keeping'.

12   An illustrated guide to the Crinan Canal, with numerous pictures of the *Linnet* is Hutton, G, *The Crinan Canal. Puffers and Paddle Steamers*, Stenlake, 1994. The same author has also published *The Crinan Canal. The Shipping Short Cut*, Stenlake, 2006. The *Linnet* served its entire working life on the canal its service ending in 1929. She was used as a club house on the Gareloch by a motor yacht society before being sunk in a storm in 1932.

13   The *Sunbeam* was especially renovated and appointed for use by Queen Victoria for her voyage through the Crinan Canal in 1847. Contemporary illustrations show that it was drawn by four horses although in her Journal,

Victoria stated that there were three. *Queen Victoria's Highland Journals*, edited by Duff, D, Lomond Books, 1994, p54.

14   The Caledonian Hotel had been newly refurbished by its owner Alexander Campbell and boasted billiard tables amongst its new amenities, a game enjoyed by Verne in his youth. The hotel was exactly opposite the North Pier at the intersection of Argyll Street and the promenade, and a mere three minute walk from the pier from which Verne was to catch the steamer the next morning. Verne was not the first famous French guest at this hotel. In 1851 the ex-queen of France, widow of Louis Philippe, took 27 rooms! Shedden, H, *The Story of Oban, Lorne and its Islands, Book III, Oban*, Oban Times Ltd, 1936. Coincidentally, she arrived in a steamer named *Dolphin*, the name Verne gave to the vessel in the *Blockade Runners*.

15   Bray, E, *The Discovery of the Hebrides. Voyagers to the Western Isles 1745–1883*, Collins, 1986.

16   Interview with Jules Verne, Jones, G, *Jules Verne at Home*, Temple Bar no. 129, 1904, 664–671

17   The *Pioneer* had been a ferry on a variety of routes but in 1875 she was lengthened and given a deck saloon to protect passengers against the weather and a second funnel, to reduce the amount of smoke affecting passengers, which made her suitable for excursion sailing around the island of Mull.

18   As in the case of Ben Lomond, Verne gives an incorrect height to Ben More. He gives an altitude of 3,500 feet whereas the actual height is only 3,171 feet.

19   An excellent account of the traditional excursion to Iona and Staffa illustrated by fascinating postcards is Charnley, B, *Iona and Staffa via Oban*, Clan Books, Doune, 1994. An evocative collection of old photographs is provided by Byron, B, *Old Iona and Staffa*, Stenlake Press, 2007.

20   The letter is conserved in the archives of the Taylor Institute Library, Oxford University, MS.F/VERNE 3.

21   He is referring to *Le Sphinx des Glaces*, 1897, which completes an unfinished book by Edgar Allan Poe and which he dedicates to the memory of Poe and to 'My American friends'.

22   He foreshadows the publication of his next book *Le testament d'un excentrique*, 1899, (*The will of an eccentric*), in which a rich American exploits a game similar to snakes and ladders in which each of the States forms one of the places in the game, in order to decide the destination of his legacy.

23 Verne is referring to the visit with his brother Paul aboard the *Great Eastern* in 1867 when he visited New York, the Hudson Valley and the Niagara Falls.

24 A summary of Verne's 1879 visit and its relationship to *The Green Ray* is Thompson, IB, 'The second visit to Scotland by Jules Verne in 1879', *Scottish Geographical Journal*, vol. 123, no. 3, 2008.

CHAPTER THREE

The 'Scottish' Novels

FOR AN AUTHOR WHO only made two short visits to the country separated by a 20 year interval the degree to which Scotland features in Verne's output is remarkable. Verne spent less than two weeks ashore in Scotland, but such were the impressions he gained and the notes that he assiduously accumulated, that his imagination enabled him to sustain the duration of his fiction substantially. In the *Fabulous Adventures of Master Antifer*, the episode in Edinburgh lasts just under two weeks. By comparison, *The Green Ray* spans a five week period. The portion of *The Children of Captain Grant* which takes place in Scotland extends to six weeks. The duration of *The Blockade Runners* from the hatching of the plot to the departure from Glasgow takes five months. The time span of *The Underground City* is less specific, but the duration is between four and five years. In addition to these five novels, he populates other stories with no fewer than 40 Scottish characters and alludes to Scottish scenes, qualities and historical events in several novels. Also remarkable is that all the five books to be presented in Part Two differ from each other greatly and represent totally contrasted literary genres.

The most logical way to present them would be by order of publication since each volume has its own specific character and they defy any grouping or ordering. The following presentation begins with *Les Forceurs de blocus* (*The Blockade Runners*), published in 1865. This is a novella, a short story rather than a full length novel in the *Voyages Extraordinaires* series. It is a beautifully constructed, fast-moving story which combines several of Verne's enthusiasms: his love of the sea and maritime challenges, the use of technology in the design of the vessel concerned, his fascination with the United States and a heroine of intelligence and determination. It is at once a story of action and romance, in which peril gives way to a happy ending. As a short novel it was unsuitable for the usual process of appearance in instalments in the children's publication the *Magasin d'Education et de Récréation* before being consolidated into a book. It was first published in the magazine *Musée des Familles* and subsequently in Hetzel's *Voyages Extraordinaires* octavo series, accompanying *Une Ville*

Flottante in a single volume. In fact, Jules Verne was contracted to Hetzel at this time to produce three volumes a year and worked simultaneously on *The Children of Captain Grant* and *The Blockade Runners*[1]. Not surprisingly, for economy of effort and to share some of the research between the two books, Glasgow and the Clyde feature prominently in both. However, whereas *The Blockade Runners* is an action-packed short story, *The Children of Captain Grant* is a tour de force of sustained adventure, which circumnavigates the world from Scotland to New Zealand and back and in which Verne revealed himself as a 'geographical' novelist *par excellence*. The novel first appeared in instalments in the *Magasin d'Education et de Récréation* in 1865 before being consolidated into three volumes in the *Voyages Extraordinaires* series in 1867. The hero, Lord Glenarvan of Luss, typifies Verne's perception of the Scottish aristocrat, tinged with a certain disdain for England, while his wife, Lady Helena, bears more than a passing resemblance to Margaret Bain in terms of charm and intelligence.

Les Indes noires (*The Underground City*) appeared over a decade later in 1877 in *Le Temps* magazine and later that year in the *Voyages Extraordinaires*. Set largely in the Trossachs, this book blends mystery, the supernatural and fear and, although it has a happy ending, it is a *roman noir*, the darkness being intensified by the fact that much of the action takes place underground. There is a political subtext in terms of visions of a utopian existence and good versus evil, but above all it is an evocative story which exploits Verne's 1859 visits to Edinburgh and the Trossachs in particular. It is a novel that can be analysed on a variety of levels: as a supernatural tale or as an allegory with a political content for example. Of the novels derived from his 1859 visit, it is the one which exploits most comprehensively his own journey. Again, it includes a heroine, Nell, the 'child of the cavern'.

The fourth novel, *The Green Ray*, published in *Le Temps* and in the *Voyages Extraordinaires* in 1882, was almost entirely based on his 1879 visit, and not, as many early biographers have suggested, his 1859 journey. Again the genre is changed and is in fact the exact opposite of the sombre *Underground City*. It is a light-hearted, humorous story with a predictable happy ending but it is distinctive in several respects. Firstly it follows Verne's 1879 visit to the Hebrides exactly down to topographic and navigational detail. Secondly, it is one of the relatively few *Voyages Extraordinaires* where the principal character is a heroine. Verne was frequently criticised for his lack of prominent female characters in his novels, but this is not true of his Scottish novels for each one features a woman, always portrayed in the most sympathetic manner, a reflection we may assume of his admiration for Margaret Bain, the only young Scottish woman he met as far as is known. Dismissed by some critics as being lightweight, *The Green Ray* has considerable charm and some fine descriptive passages. Hetzel, by the time of its publication an increasingly critical and interfering publisher, approved of it. It is also firmly anchored in Verne's personal experience rather than extensive research of second hand sources. Finally, *The Fabulous Adventures of Master Antifer*, published in episodes in *Le Magasin d'Education et de Récréation* and in the *Voyages Extraordinaires* series in 1894, includes chapters set in Edinburgh. Again, the genre differs from the previous books. It involves several of Verne's favourite themes: his taste for mysteries based on cryptic clues and his disdain in his later years for wealth and its corrupting power. The story is based on an international treasure hunt guided by clues in which the episode in Edinburgh features the denunciation of material wealth by a fundamentalist Free Church of Scotland minister, who pays for this stance by being violently physically attacked. The Scottish passage is thus a scene of greed, violence and betrayal, but the villains are foreign rather than Scots!

There are difficulties in citing consistent dates and editions of Verne's novels for several reasons. Firstly, as mentioned above, his novels were initially published in instalments in magazines and especially *Le Magasin illustré d'Education et de Récréation*, and only after the last episode were they consolidated into books by his publisher Hetzel. Secondly, Verne was an inveterate reviser of his manuscripts. He not only scribbled changes and corrections to his handwritten manuscripts but also made substantial changes at the stage of the printer's proofs. Moreover, Hetzel also enforced changes to plots and characters, at times to Verne's annoyance. Neither is it always possible to refer to English translations on a consistent basis. Some of the early translations were of poor quality or bowdlerised, while others were abridged and simplified to make them accessible to children. In these circumstances, and in the interests of consistency, the versions of Verne's novels preferred in the preparation of this book are the integral illustrated octavo volumes produced by Hetzel in the *Voyages Extraordinaires* Series.

A pen and ink sketch of Jules Verne, attributed to Harry Furniss, pictured apparently correcting proofs in his bedroom study in Amiens, late 19th century.
National Portrait Gallery, London

Verne has often been referred to as the founder of science fiction and linked in this sense with H.G. Wells. Other reviewers have modified this view to consider him as an author of novels of 'anticipation'. In fact, in his lifetime Verne rejected both of these views of his work, considering

The entrance to *La Société de Géographie de Paris* on the *Boulevard St-Germain*, showing on either side of the globe, classical figures representing land and sea. Verne was a member of the society and gave a lecture there on the international dateline, a crucial element in his novel *Around the World in Eighty Days*.
Société de Géographie de Paris

that all of his writing was based on solid contemporary evidence of what form future developments might take. Thus we find no 'little green men' in his novels and in general the futuristic elements are based on reading scientific journals complemented by help from professional scientists, mathematicians and engineers. In truth, his Scottish novels correspond much more closely to what he himself considered to be his distinctive genre, the 'geographical novel', a format warmly encouraged by Hetzel since it suited his magazine's educational objectives and moreover was highly profitable.

Verne had been enthusiastic about geography since his school days and in 1865 he became member number 710 of the *Société de Géographie de Paris*, the oldest geographical society in the world, founded in 1821. This afforded him three major advantages. He was able to consult the Society's vast collection of books, journals, maps and atlases. Secondly, he was able to indulge one of his greatest enthusiasms, reading the reports of scientific explorations of exotic realms in, for example, the high Arctic and interior Africa. Thirdly, by attending the Society's meetings he met some of the most influential scientists, geographers and explorers of his day. In an interview with Marie Belloc in 1895, Verne explained:

> I have always been devoted to the study of geography, much as some people delight in history and historical research. I really think that my love of maps and the great explorers led to my composing the first of my long series of geographical stories[2].

In this format, two main inspirations are detectable. Verne followed avidly the great maritime and overland expeditions which were increasing knowledge of extreme environments and exotic societies. He was, for example, fully aware of the expeditions of the great Scottish explorers David Livingstone and Mungo Park. Secondly he was fascinated by the expansion of empires and the issues raised by the colonial experience. The phenomenon of colonisation by the European powers and the imperial process exercised Verne's conscience considerably and formed the framework of several of his novels. The British Empire in particular absorbed his imagination. On the one hand he admired the efficiency of the British colonial process, but as a man with a hatred of violence, he abhorred the ruthless and bloody manner in which many parts of the Empire were acquired and subdued. Some contradictions are apparent in the sense that he held 'English' colonialism in disdain and yet approved of Scottish attempts to found colonies[3]. He also conveniently overlooked the fact that many of the explorers, missionaries, administrators, entrepreneurs and the military in the creation of the British Empire were in fact Scots!

The *Voyages Extraordinaires* in effect conceptualised a new genre of fiction. While essentially adventure stories, they nevertheless had a solid basis in the geography of the areas in which the plots evolved. Verne did not hesitate at times to contact geographers and scientists directly for advice on the authenticity of these geographies[4]. His study in Amiens was filled with thousands of classified notes based on his extensive research. In the case of his Scottish novels it is clear that he made copious notes and sketches of his travels to provide local detail, using the geographer's eye for observation of the landscape, people and topography. Sadly these notes have been lost, or if they still exist are not in the public domain. If Verne may be considered to have invented the 'geographical' novel, without the involvement of his publisher Hetzel this particular genre may not have achieved its fullest expression. The format of Verne's novels were, ideally suited the format of the *Magasin d'Education et de Récréation*. They were easily divided into episodes and fulfilled Hetzel's intention of providing a magazine which was instructive in a pedagogical sense, suitable for family consumption, Republican and non-religious in content and very profitable, not least to Hetzel himself. Verne was the inventor of the geographical novel; Hetzel was its promoter and publicist. It is no coincidence that many of the first or early editions that have survived and are available in the second-hand book trade were originally school prizes.

Although Verne had the geographer's skill of describing landscape, it cannot be claimed that all of his observations were original. Scotland was an increasingly favourite destination of travellers during the Romantic period. The country had been remote, relatively inaccessible except by strenuous effort, but its scenery and folklore were an inspiration to writers, poets, artists and musicians[5]. Verne did not conceal the fact that, especially in his 1859 visit, he relied on travel guides to provide background detail. In some instances he not only 'borrowed' descriptions but actually incorporated elements into his plots. This especially applies to the travelogue by Nodier, which provided Verne with information on Edinburgh and The Trossachs in particular and may well have inspired episodes in *Les Indes noires*[6]. A rather forgotten novel by Nodier published in the same year, *Trilby, ou le Lutin d'Argyll* (*Trilby or the fairy of Argyll*), 1822, may well have supplied Verne with material concerning the supernatural spirits which populated the Trossachs. The travel guides to Scotland by Joanne and Enault also offered Verne the kind of local geographical and historical detail that provided the background substance to his novels. In fact, such was the attraction of Scotland during the first half of the nineteenth century that dozens of accounts were published by French travellers and Verne may well have been familiar with some of them[7].

In addition to geographical guides and travel accounts, Verne had immersed himself in Scott's novels and was also versed in ancient myths and legends. His frequent evocations of the poetry of Ossian, especially in connection with the legends of Fingal, exemplify his fascination with Scotland's dim and distant past[8]. In effect, Verne was enraptured by the visions of Scotland portrayed in Europe by the Romantic Movement, and Scott's novels and poems were widely translated and admired in France. The myth of the 'noble savage' as embodied by the Highlander, with traditional dress, bearing arms and striding out to the skirl of the bagpipes stirred Verne deeply. The evocative paintings of Turner and Landseer and the poetry of Wordsworth and Coleridge were landmarks, as was the music of Mendelssohn. Hans Christian Anderson had already followed Verne's 1859 route almost exactly in 1847[9]. An enormous boost to the image of the Highlands as an area no longer to be regarded as remote and uncivilised, especially south of the border, was Queen Victoria's delight in visiting Scotland and the purchase of her estate and castle at Balmoral. By 1850, Thomas Cook had established tours of the Trossachs via Loch Lomond, Inversnaid and Loch Katrine, and with the introduction of steamers on the lochs and the spread of railways, by the time Verne made his first journey, the Highlands were no longer as isolated and gloomy as pictured in Samuel Johnson and James Boswell's diaries[10]. He was thus able in the space of a few days to experience much of the setting of Scott's novels, made possible by the integration of transport systems sadly lacking today.

In spite of the incorporation of 'derived' material into many of Verne's novels, it is in the case of his Scottish stories that he most exploits his own first-hand experience and also his personal engagement with a country and a people that he so admired. The individual studies which now follow are intended as commentaries rather than literary criticism. They are summaries of the plots and personnae in sufficient detail to demonstrate Verne's perceptions of Scotland, but also to encourage the reader to enjoy the novels in full.

Notes

1   In total, Verne published 62 *Voyages Extraordinaires*, including all of the Scottish novels except for *The Blockade Runners*, which is a novella. Although Verne was contracted to Hetzel initially to deliver three volumes per annum, later reduced to two, this did not require three separate novels. *The Children of Captain Grant*, for example, was delivered in three separate volumes.

2   Belloc, MA, *Jules Verne at Home*, Strand Magazine, 1895. His interest in geography is also evidenced in his classic *Twenty Thousand Leagues under the Sea* in which Captain Nemo includes in the library of his submarine, the *Nautilus*, classic geographical texts together with the 'Bulletins of diverse geographical societies'.

3   He may have been aware of the disastrous attempt to found a Scottish colony in Darian in the isthmus of Panama in 1698. This is echoed in the failure of Captain Grant's attempt to found a colony in *The Children of Captain Grant*.

4   An example is provided by the Russian émigré geographer Kropotkin whom it has been suggested Verne possibly met in Paris and who may have provided him with background detail for Verne's novel *Michel Strogoff*, one of his most successful books, which was transformed into a long-running stage play.

5   A striking comparison with Verne's first visit to Scotland was that made by the German poet and philosopher Theodor Fontane. He had a travelling companion, visited Scotland the summer before Verne and followed an almost identical circuit in the Highlands. He published the journal of the journey which was translated in an English edition as *Across the Tweed. Notes on Travel in Scotland, 1858*, Phoenix House, London, 1965. Unlike Verne, he shows less interest in landscape and folklore and much more in battlegrounds, history and architecture.

6   Charles Nodier, *Promenade de Dieppe aux montagnes d'Ecosse*, Paris, Barba, 1821.

PART TWO

The Scottish Fiction
of Jules Verne

CHAPTER FOUR

The Blockade Runners

THE AMERICAN CIVIL WAR began on 12 April 1861, when Confederate troops opened fire on the Federal garrison of Fort Sumter at the mouth of Charleston Harbour, South Carolina. A city of some 40,000 inhabitants and a major port for the export of cotton produced by the slave system of the rich plantation owners, Charleston was the birthplace of the attempt at secession by the Southern States from the Federal Union. In Glasgow reactions to the war were mixed. On the one hand, frequent public meetings – usually organised by the churches, especially the women members – were held condemning slavery. On the other, the blockade of the southern cotton exporting ports, like Charleston, Savannah and New Orleans, was strangling the city's textile industry to death. It is estimated that in 1857 200,000 people were employed in textile factories in Glasgow[1]. The shortage of raw cotton resulted in the closure of mills and tens of thousands being thrown out of work. The textile industry was almost entirely based on cotton and the sole source was the American South. The crisis was all the more acute in that Glasgow produced high value items like muslin and embroidered cloth and the loss of this profitable activity meant that the factory owners suffered and closures were widespread. Objections to slavery on moral grounds were thus tempered by the misery of working class factory workers. Moreover, the 'barons' of the textile mills were only too aware of the fate of their predecessors, the 'Tobacco Lords', deprived of their imports of raw tobacco by the American War of Independence. Ironically, as the Civil War progressed a new market opened up for Glasgow's entrepreneurs.

In addition to hampering the export of cotton, the blockade also compromised the import of armaments and consumer goods into the Southern States. Arms were needed to pursue the war while wealthy plantation owners were deprived of imported high quality goods to sustain their gracious style of living. A market demand therefore existed for the purchase of sea-going vessels capable of breaking through the Northerners' blockade. Initially this demand was met by the sale of existing Clyde paddle steamers, though built for the sheltered waters of the Firth of Clyde some did not survive the Atlantic Ocean crossing. When this supply dried up, Confederate agents turned to ordering new ships. There was a need for fast vessels with a shallow draught, capable of out-running the blockading ships and penetrating the shallow water of estuary channels inaccessible to the larger Northern ships. Glasgow's shipyards eagerly filled this profitable market in which speed of construction was more important to the Confederate agents than price.

The Northerners were aware of the threat of modern ships to the effectiveness of the blockade. For example if we consult the log of John B Marchand, who commanded the USS *James Adger* in 1862 (the date when the fictional *Dolphin* was being built in Glasgow), a picture emerges of vain attempts to capture or sink blockade runners and even to intercept them in the Western Approaches of the English Channel. An epilogue to his diary states:

> Part of the reason for the inefficiency of the blockade was the poor condition of the blockading vessels. But another reason was that the blockade runners grew increasingly skilful. They were no longer amateurs hoping to run through the blockade in privately owned sailing barks. The men who now navigated the channels off Charleston were professional blockade runners in specially designed steamships, painted gray to blend with the sea at night. They were cunning and swift and knew their trade[2].

It was against this context that Jules Verne wrote *The Blockade Runners*. The European press covered the Civil War in great detail either by its own correspondents or by syndicating reports published in the American Press. Thus Verne was able to follow events in the war with little more than a week's delay. If we consider the case of Scotland's leading news-paper, *The Scotsman*, in the year of 1862, the starting date of Verne's novel and when the war was gaining pace, coverage of the progress of the war was frequent and detailed. Every week contained one or more reports, editorials or letters to the editor. The war correspondents were mainly employees of New York papers, but articles were also published from, for example, the *Richmond Examiner* and the *St Louis Democrat*. Characteristically, these syndicated articles appeared 10 to 14 days after publication in America. An example of the kind of detail which reached *The Scotsman* is provided by a whole broadsheet page article published on Saturday 11 January 1862 entitled 'The Destruction of Charleston Harbour by the Federal Stone Fleet' by the correspondent of the *New York Times* writing from 'Off Charleston' on 21 December 1861[3]. This gives a very detailed account of the sinking of 16 stone-filled hulks (mainly old whaling ships) in the Main Ship Channel of the harbour on 19 December to blockade the port. In fact this was a useless exercise as marine life rapidly decomposed the wooden hulls and the stone blocks sank beneath the mud. If a small, but very literate, nation like Scotland should have had access to such detailed reports, Verne would surely have found an abundance of material in French newspapers and journals. Furthermore, he would have been able to consult the *Société de Géographie de Paris,* which held an extensive collection of maps, to locate action in the various theatres of the war and possibly to have access to charts of Charleston Harbour.

In addition to this research, Verne could also draw on his own experience for the Scottish setting of the novella. In 1859, he had travelled by coach from Glasgow Bridge and the Broomielaw along the quays of the northern shore, probably as far as Partick, before returning to the city centre via the Park District. He would thus have traversed the length of Glasgow Harbour with its shipyards, its engine works like Napier's yard, and all the ancillary industries of shipbuilding such as timber working, rope and sail making. He did not see at first hand the lower Clyde and the Firth until his 1879 journey, although he would have had good visibility of the stretch as far as Dumbarton from the train in 1859 as he made his way to Balloch and Loch Lomond. The detail of this area was probably researched from travel guides and possibly maritime charts. This material was exploited in both *The Blockade Runners* and in *The Children of Captain Grant,* the two books overlapping in production. Armed with the notes of his 1859 visit and copious research, Verne picked up his pen as the four years of the bloody Civil War were drawing to an exhausted end to produce a story which is authentic and exciting in equal measure.

The plot is hatched and the 'Dolphin' is born

The story begins on 3 December 1862, when after over a year of warfare, the effect of the blockade had begun to ruin Glasgow's textile industry. A huge crowd had gathered on both banks of the Clyde to witness a ship

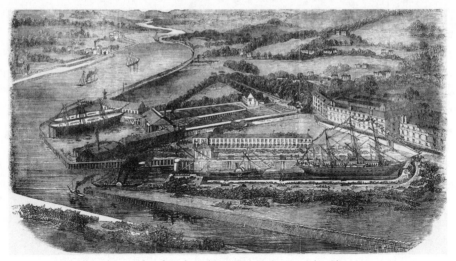

The shipyards of Tod and McGregor in Partick, Glasgow,
where the *Dolphin* was built.
Illustrated London News

launch from the yards of Tod and McGregor at the confluence of the
Clyde and its tributary the Kelvin[4]. A ship launch was an everyday event
along the Clyde, but the launch of the *Dolphin*[5] had attracted both
enthusiasm and curiosity. She was equipped with powerful engines from
Lancefield Quay and twin screws which could operate independently to
give great manoeuverability[6]. Although 1,500 tons, she had a shallow
draught and it was clear to the more knowledgeable in the crowd gathered
on both the Partick and Govan banks that here was a vessel capable of high
speed from her powerful engines and three sail masts. She had the capacity
to make abrupt changes in course and could navigate in shallow water[7].
The general conjecture was that the *Dolphin* was headed for a role in the
Civil War, but the precise nature of this was a matter of speculation.

To discover the secret of the *Dolphin's* mission, Verne takes the reader
back five months to the coffee room of the Tontine Hotel on Glasgow's
Trongate[8]. Here Verne draws on his 1859 experience since, after his
fruitless visit to the closed cathedral, he had made his way by coach along
the main streets of the city centre, including the Trongate on which the
hotel with its impressive façade stood. Verne describes the location of the
coffee room exactly, situated under the arcades of the hotel and next to
the town hall. As well as being in one of the most important hotels in

The Tontine Hotel Glasgow where the plot to force the blockade was hatched.
The 'Tontine Faces' are visible at the apex of each arch.
Mitchell Library Glasgow

the city, the Tontine coffee room was a commercial institution in its own right. Each morning the commercial and business leaders of the city would gather here to consult business reports and the daily papers, including papers from France. Strangers were unwelcome in this nerve centre of the city's commercial economy. In the privacy of the room, information could be exchanged and deals struck, but above all, the progress of the American war and its impact on Glasgow's trade and industry was the dominant topic of conversation in the summer of 1862. This indeed was the subject of a discreet conversation between a 50 year old ship owner and merchant, Vincent Playfair, and his 30 year old nephew James Playfair, an experienced and dashing captain of merchant ships[9].

The blockade had seriously compromised the Playfair family business, but James confided to his uncle that he had a plan to break through the blockade and at the same time to make a substantial profit. Two elements were involved in the plan. Firstly, James would captain a new and specially designed ship, which as we have already seen was to be the *Dolphin*.

Secondly, the blockade was to be broken at Charleston, South Carolina. Here the Confederate garrison under the command of General Beauregard was encircled by the Union troops and was desperately in need of arms and provisions. At the same time the city's warehouses were bulging with cotton which could be acquired at a minimal cost. The secret plan was agreed between the two and an order for the construction of the ship was placed with Tod and McGregor to be delivered in December, when the long winter nights would give James Playfair the advantage of darkness to force the blockade[10].

Sea trials and preparations for sailing

The *Dolphin* passed her sea trials in the Firth of Clyde with flying colours, attaining a speed of 17 sea miles an hour. Satisfied that she could outrun the Union ships, James Playfair returned to the Steamboat Quay and the loading of arms, consumer goods and coal commenced[11]. James Playfair carefully selected a crew but at the last minute a well-built man approached him and pleaded to be engaged as a crewman. The determination and his evident physical strength persuaded Playfair to enlist this man, named Crockston, who insisted that his 'nephew', John Stiggs, should also be engaged as a trainee crewman. Anxious to set sail, Playfair agreed and on 3 January 1863, the *Dolphin* cast off her moorings and descended the Clyde.

Verne gives a detailed and accurate description of the ship's progress through the harbour, passing open country below Partick, following the dredged channel marked by stone towers[12]. The *Dolphin* passed in turn Renfrew, the Forth and Clyde Canal at Bowling at the foot of the Kilpatrick Hills and the rock on which stood Dumbarton Castle[13]. On the left bank, the *Dolphin's* wake rocked the boats in Port Glasgow before passing Greenock, the home of James Watt, whose improvements to steam engines had facilitated the mechanisation of steam navigation. By now she had entered the broad waters of the Firth of Clyde with the island of Arran visible on the horizon. She rounded the Mull of Kintyre and after dropping off the pilot into his cutter, James Playfair, now in command, made for the North Channel and out into the open Atlantic. The perilous adventure, which had taken six months to plan and prepare, was now irrevocably engaged.

Crockston unmasked

The *Dolphin* sailed westwards at full power, but this uneventful progress was soon to be disturbed by an astonishing revelation. Crockston displayed total incompetence as a sailor and James Playfair, suspecting an infiltrator, ordered his baggage to be searched. Amongst his possessions letters bearing Federal stamps were found and Crockston was exposed not only as an American, but as a supporter, in Playfair's eyes, of the hated Northern anti-slavery camp. Immediately, a flogging with the cat o' nine tails was ordered, but before the lashing could commence the young John Stiggs rushed up to James Playfair and begged to speak to him in private. In fact, the demeanour of the 'boy' had already raised suspicions in Playfair's mind and he addressed her as 'Miss' as he bade her to enter his cabin. His hunch proved to be correct, as thus challenged, 'John Stiggs' revealed her true identity. She was Jenny Halliburtt, daughter of a Northern journalist being held prisoner in Charleston. The unusual surname may have been based on that of Sir Walter Scott's grandmother, Halburton. Verne was very familiar with Scott's background, as in addition to being a famous Scot much admired by Verne, he also had a French wife, Charlotte Charpentier.

Crockston was a family servant devoted to Jenny's father and determined to rescue him from the clutches of General Beauregard in command of the garrison[14]. Verne thus introduces a second plot in addition to the blockade running attempt. Crockston and Jenny had inveigled themselves into the crew in an attempt to rescue her father and return him to the safety of Britain. The initial reaction of James Playfair was one of fury and an adherence to the cause of the Southerners. Jenny, in spite of her young age was a potent advocate of the rightfulness of the Northern attempt to reunite the States and to abolish slavery. Moreover, her skill in argument and her evident personal courage allied to her charm were beginning to undermine the resolve of Playfair and to soften his heart. As the voyage progressed Jenny never left his side and he decided to aid the rescue attempt, though without sacrificing the real purpose of the *Dolphin's* voyage. Two events further strengthened his admiration for the young girl. A Federal cruiser, the *Iroquois*, sighted the *Dolphin* and was bearing down on her. The *Dolphin* was lightly armed and relied on her speed to make her escape. The *Iroquois* fired her canons but gradually the

As the crew prepare to flog Crockston, 'John Stiggs' decides to confess her true identity as Jenny Halliburtt.

J. Férat

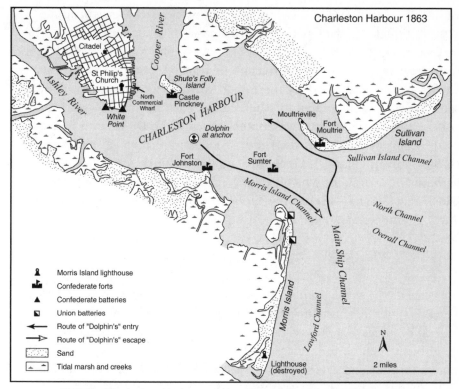

FIG. 7 Charleston Harbour at the time of *The Blockade Runners*

Dolphin sped out of range and proceeded on her course. Throughout this attack Jenny had remained beside Playfair, refusing his plea to return to her cabin. Two days later, abreast of the Bermudas, the *Dolphin* was hit by a violent squall. Wisdom dictated that she should seek shelter in the British possession, but James Playfair had confidence in his ship's ability to ride out the storm. Again Jenny never left his side even at the height of the tempest and James' admiration was rapidly turning to love.

Running the blockade

On the morning of 13 January, the American mainland was sighted and the lighthouse at the entrance to Charleston Harbour identified[15]. The *Dolphin* had been spotted by two Federal frigates which began shadowing her. At this point, Verne displays incredibly accurate information on the coastal geography of the harbour and the various channels leading to the port. Equally, he was aware of the disposition of the forts occupied by the rival troops. On the basis of this knowledge he was able to devise a strategy for Playfair to employ, to confound the opposing warships. James Playfair initially followed a course southwards which would eventually bring his ship within range of the Federal batteries on Morris Island, and the guarding frigates were content to leave the *Dolphin* to her fate. He then abruptly reversed the rudder to steam northwards and headed for the Sullivan Channel. Once through the channel safety was assured by the shallow draught which excluded the Federal ships and raising the British flag Playfair steered the *Dolphin* to her mooring place on the North Commercial Wharf. [FIG. 7]

The liberation of Jonathan Halliburtt

No sooner had the *Dolphin* moored than an excited crowd gathered. James Playfair lost no time in meeting the Confederate Commander, General Beauregard, to negotiate the sale of his cargo and to purchase bales of cotton at rock bottom prices. James took advantage of this meeting to enquire casually concerning the fate of Jenny's father, Jonathan Halliburtt. He learned that he was incarcerated in the Citadel and that within a few days he would be shot. James passed this news to Crockston, who immediately began to formulate an escape plan and to reassure the inconsolable Jenny. Playfair was to complain to Beauregard that he had a violent trouble maker aboard the *Dolphin* and requested that he should be locked up in the Citadel awaiting the sailing at which time the said villain would be re-embarked to face justice in Britain. Beauregard agreed and Crockston was led in chains to the Citadel. He would not reveal the detail of his plan, but merely asked Playfair to land at White Point in the ship's gig and to wait until 9pm on 22 January. Meanwhile, the *Dolphin* continued to load her cargo of cotton until on the afternoon of the appointed day she slipped her moorings and anchored two miles offshore in the main channel to await departure on the high tide. In the evening, after giving orders to raise steam, James Playfair slipped into the gig and the six crew members rowed as silently as possible to White Point to await the appointed hour. As the church of St Philip[16] struck 9pm, a cloaked figure approached. It was Jonathan Halliburtt followed

Jenny collapses into the arms of her rescued father.
J Férat

soon after by Crockston. Once aboard the gig, the sailors rowed mightily for the *Dolphin*, obscured by the darkness and a dense mist. Crockston explained that he had knocked out the gaoler when he brought him his evening meal, then stealing his keys and had released Halliburtt. As they approached the *Dolphin*, shots rang out from the Citadel, answered by further shots from Fort Sumter. The escape had been discovered! Once aboard, Jenny flung herself into her father's arms in tears while Captain Playfair urged his stokers to raise maximum steam. The *Dolphin* sped toward the Morris Island Channel, a surprising and daring route which placed her briefly in the line of fire from Fort Sumter and then the Morris Island Fort[17].

Passing this danger with only slight damage, the next hazard was an approaching frigate which attempted to block the *Dolphin's* passage. At once Playfair shut down one of the screws and the ship executed an abrupt change of course on the other propeller.

This unexpected diversion gave the *Dolphin* an advantage and it now remained for her to out-run the frigate to the open sea. It took one last act of heroism from Crockston to achieve this. A shell from a pursuing gun boat landed on the foredeck of the *Dolphin* and threatened to blow her up. Crockston rushed forward and with his great strength managed to lift the shell and hurl it into the sea where it exploded violently but harmlessly. By now the ship had reached the safety of the open sea and reached Glasgow after a smooth crossing. The main event was that James Playfair, by now overcome with love for Jenny, proposed marriage to her, which she joyfully accepted. The novella ends on a note of happiness. James and Jenny were married in St Mungo's cathedral on 14 February followed by a lavish banquet at Vincent Playfair's home in Gordon Street. For nephew and uncle the *Dolphin's* cargo could not have been better. The most valuable item of cargo for James was Jenny herself, while his uncle had a cargo of cotton that raised a profit of 375 per cent!

The Blockade Runners is a superbly constructed novella. It commences energetically in Glasgow with the launch of the *Dolphin* and with dual plots, that of Vincent and James Playfair and simultaneously that of Crockston and Jenny. A crescendo of action is reached as the blockade is run, Jonathan Halliburtt is rescued and the blockade penetrated again. The return crossing is tranquil to be followed by the joyous ending of the wedding in Glasgow. On the surface it is a straightforward but imaginative

With his immense strength Crockston hurls the shell overboard in the nick of time.
J Férat

Rewards all round! James Playfair gains a wife and Vincent Playfair gains
a handsome profit.

J Férat

story, based on accurate historical and geographical details researched by Verne and which gives conviction to the action. Beneath the plot, however, Verne raises issues which he found troubling. For example the intense conversations between James and Jenny on the subject of slavery have been taken to suggest that at this stage of his life Verne was ambivalent on the slave system and in particular the freedom of the Confederate States to secede from the Union[18]. In fact, Verne became a convinced opponent of slavery, the horrors of which were expounded in a later novel, *Un capitaine de quinze ans*, 1878, published under a number of names in English translations of which *Dick Sands, the Boy Captain*, the name of the hero, is the most usual. Even more emphatically, an entire novel, *Nord contre Sud*, 1885 (*North Against South*) features a plantation owner in Florida who frees his slaves during the middle of the Civil War. Nevertheless, in *The Blockade Runners*, Verne might be accused of sacrificing reference to the carnage and horror of the Civil War land battles in favour of a stirring, largely maritime, adventure.

Similarly, the motivation of greed for wealth, implicit in the trade of arms for cotton, was a theme which recurred in Verne's writing particularly towards the end of his life. Finally, *The Blockade Runners* was a precursor of a series of novels set in North America. While never exclusively replacing Scotland in Verne's spiritual affection, he became increasingly admiring of the energy, technology and initiative of the United States, especially after his visit to the States in 1867. This admiration was nevertheless tempered by disdain for the propensity for progress to be motivated and measured by wealth accumulation.

Notes

1 *Third Statistical Account of Scotland*, Glasgow, 1958, 240–264. Verne fails to recognise that Scots had played a major role in the slave trade, especially in Jamaica and the Leeward Islands, as plantation owners and merchants.

2 John B Marchand, *Charleston blockade; the journals of John B. Marchand, US Navy, 1861–62*, Naval War College Press, Newport, 1976.

3 *The Scotsman*, 11 January 1862.

4   Tod and McGregor's shipyard existed in reality and it is likely that Verne saw it in 1859. It was situated at the confluence of the Clyde and the Kelvin, on the right bank of the Kelvin known as Meadowside. In fact at the time when Verne was writing, both of the founders were dead, Tod died in 1858 and McGregor in 1859, and the shipyard was run by their sons, 25 and 18 years old respectively. It was the first shipyard on the Clyde to feature a dry dock. Riddell, J, *The Clyde. The Making of a River*, John Donald, Edinburgh, 1979, p135.

   McGregor lived virtually on the shipyard site, but Tod lived in Partickhill in a villa, recently demolished for the construction of new flats, linked to the Clyde by a steep footpath still known in Partick, to older generations at least, as 'Tod's Brae'. Appropriately the shipyard site is now under redevelopment to create a major transport museum in which the shipbuilding and maritime legacy of the Clyde will be featured prominently.

5   In his manuscript and in French editions of the novella, Verne names the ship the *Delphin*. This is the German word for dolphin and as Verne had no competence in English either he made a simple error or his notoriously difficult handwriting was misread by the printer and was uncorrected by Verne. Moreover, in the illustrations to the French text, the lifebelts of the boat are clearly marked in French as *Dauphin*. In the original manuscript, held at the *Centre d'études verniennes* in Nantes, the title of the first chapter is headed *The Duncan* which he then erased and substituted *Delphin*. This suggests that he had contemplated using a Scottish name for the ship, but he used this name for Lord Glenarvan's yacht in *The Children of Captain Grant* instead. Given these contradictions in this book the name *Dolphin* is adhered to as there is no apparent reason to use the German name. Within a few hundred metres of Tod and McGregor's shipyard is an old inn named the *Dolphin* which exists to this day. This seems to be a coincidence and results from the fact that a local choir in Partick named *The Dolphin* used to rehearse in this building.

6   Verne's reference to the twin screw design as being built by 'Dudgeon of Milwal' [sic] was based on accurate fact. This company existed at Millwall Wharf on the Isle of Dogs, the heart of London's docklands in the 19th century. Dudgeon's Yard was adjacent to the yard of John Scott Russell, which built the *Leviathan* seen by Verne in 1859 and which later, as the *Great Eastern*, transported Verne and his brother to New York in 1867.

7   Verne describes the engines as having been manufactured by Napier at Lancefield Forge. This company was synonymous with excellence in marine engine design manufacture. It would have been normal practice for

ships to have been launched as hulls and towed to Lancefield Quay where the Forge had a quay with powerful steam cranes which could lower engines and boilers into the hull. Verne's account is rather ambiguous on this point. The *Dolphin* is launched with engines already fitted and sets sail for sea trials almost immediately. The magnificent aerial sketch of the Tod and McGregor shipyard published in the *Illustrated London News* of 29 January 1858 shows no sign of a steam crane and so how the *Dolphin* received its Napier engines is unclear. An account of Napier's engineering activity is included in Wood, J, *Scottish Engineering. The Machine Makers,* NMS Publishing Ltd., 2000. A comprehensive history of shipbuilding on the Clyde from its earliest times is provided by Walker, F M, *Song of the Clyde. A History of Clyde Shipbuilding,* John Donald, Edinburgh, 2001, 247pp.

8   The Tontine Hotel was named after Lorenzo Tonti, a Neapolitan banker who devised the Tontine investment system in France in 1853. The system involved a group of investors whose assets were distributed to the surviving members of the group on their death rather than being part of the person's estate. Thus the last surviving member received the total assets of the investment. The system was eventually declared illegal because of the incentive to engineer the untimely death of the participants, a process exploited by R L Stevenson in his novel *The Wrong Box* (1889). A popular choice of Tontine investment in Scotland was in hotels and the name 'Tontine' survives, for example in hotels in Peebles and Greenock and elsewhere. The Glasgow Tontine Hotel was built originally as a town hall with an arcaded plaza, the arches of which were surmounted by gargoyle-like faces. It was bought by the Tontine Society in 1781 and extended as the Tontine Hotel and Coffee Room. In 1869 it was converted to a drapers' shop and was subsequently demolished. All that remains of the hotel are some of the carved faces which were the keystones of the arches of the arcade and which are conserved in the garden of Provand's Lordship Museum, the oldest house in Glasgow. Remarkably, a large new office block in Gordon Street is named 'Tontine House'. The building has an arcaded façade and reproductions of the 'Tontine Faces' have been incorporated.

9   The name 'Playfair' seems to be totally fictitious possibly to avoid any legal consequences though it has been suggested that a good fit would be The Albion Trading Company.

10   Examination of Tod and McGregor's ship building list in Glasgow University's Library's Business Archive collection indicates that the company never built a vessel named the *Dolphin* which is thus a fictitious name. The only reference to a blockade runner built on the Clyde with the name *Dolphin* was a paddle

steamer built in 1844 by Napier. She was disposed of to Liverpool owners in 1862 who promptly sold her to American Confederate agents as reported in *The Clyde Passenger Steamers*, Davies, K, Kyle Publications, Ayr, 1980. Authoritative sources concerning the acquisition of blockade-busting vessels are, Wise, Stephen, *Lifeline of the Confederacy. Blockade Running during the Civil War*, University of South Carolina Press, 1988, and more recently, Graham, EJ, *Clyde Built. Blockade Runners, Cruisers and Armoured Rams of the American Civil War*, Birlinn, Edinburgh, 2006. A vessel of note built by Tod and McGregor in 1862 was the *Lady Nyasa*, built for the explorer David Livingstone and transported to Africa in sections.

11 Steamboat Quay, where the *Dolphin* was provisioned, later became Anderston Quay and subsequently part of the Broomielaw, the main departure point of steamers. When it was constructed, the cost was paid by a tax of one sixth of a penny on every pint of beer consumed in Glasgow! 'Steamboat Quay' was also a generic term with the same nomenclature being applied at Stirling and Greenock at that time.

12 These stone towers, which Verne refers to as 'biggins' and which still exist, would have been fully visible to him in 1859 from the train to Balloch.

13 Here Verne makes one of several errors of altitude in his Scottish novels. He refers to the castle as being at 400 feet whereas in fact it is only at 100 feet.

14 The French name of General Beauregard reflects his créole origin; he was born in New Orleans in 1818 and was appointed General in charge of the Charleston garrison in 1861. He was a dashing, if somewhat rash, commander.

15 Here Verne's knowledge of local detail is inaccurate. The lighthouse, on Morris Island, in common with all the lights from Virginia to Texas, had been extinguished by the Confederates in 1861 and the mechanism removed to prevent incursions by Northern vessels. Moreover, the Morris Island lighthouse had been completely demolished in 1862 in order to prevent the Northern Army using it as a watchtower overlooking Fort Sumter.

16 St Phillip's Church is still a familiar landmark of Charleston. With the destruction of the Morris Island lighthouse, a light was installed in the church tower to guide vessels through the harbour to the docks.

17 The Morris Island Channel no longer exists as a navigable route due to siltation and infilling by material dredged to maintain the deep channel to the port and naval base, and sandbanks are exposed at low tide. Although modern Charleston has been transformed by port expansion and urban

development, the historic core is remarkably well preserved as are the forts in the harbour and on the shore. The present day visitor has no difficulty in recognising most of the features mentioned by Verne.

18 The fact that the initial prosperity of the port of Nantes was in part based on the slave trade, and that, as legal advisers to shippers, some of the previous owners of Verne's father's practice may indirectly have participated in this trade, may have coloured the ambivalent attitude to slavery that Verne expresses via the Playfairs. It seems that Verne's initial hostility to the Southern States was based on his antipathy to the break-up of the Union to a greater extent than sympathy with the Abolitionist cause. However, his opposition to slavery became progressively stronger and explicit in several of his later novels.

CHAPTER FIVE

The Children of Captain Grant

LES ENFANTS DU CAPITAINE GRANT, 1868 (*The Children of Captain Grant*) is Verne's 'geographical' novel par excellence and a three volume 'blockbuster'. The novel begins and ends in Glasgow, but the rest of the book is written on a global scale and the 'Scottish' element resides mainly in the characters, rather than the setting. The main personalities are Lord Glenarvan and his new wife Lady Helena, residents of Malcolm Castle in Luss on the shore of Loch Lomond. There is no record of a Glenarvan on Lomondside, nor is there a Malcolm Castle. The Malcolm Clan did not have its base on Lomondside. Its headquarters is at Duntrune Castle, north of Crinan on the Atlantic coast.

Lord Glenarvan is more than likely modelled on the Colquhoun clan. The Colquhoun lands were granted by Malcolm, Earl of Lennox to Humphrey of Kilpatrick in the 13th century and he adopted Colquhoun as the clan name. 'Malcolm' castle can thus be proposed as being Rossdhu House, near Luss, the head quarters of the Colquhoun Clan, which also contains a ruined medieval castle and chapel in the grounds. Verne had sailed past Rossdhu House in 1859 as the steamer approached the pier at Luss. In 1879 he sailed past Luss from the opposite direction and his diary for that day makes specific mention of Malcolm Castle and Lord Glenarvan. Moreover, it is clear from a reference in *Les Indes noires*, that he was aware of the association of the Colquhoun clan with Luss. He may also have been aware that Helensburgh, a planned town built in 1780 by Sir James Colquhoun, was named after his wife Helen and therefore a possible origin of Verne's Lady Helena.

Lord Glenarvan typified Verne's notion of the Scottish nobleman. He is portrayed as being utterly loyal to his staff, all of whom were born and bred locally, who in turn give him their unreserved respect. Although a peer in the House of Lords and a member of the Royal Thames Yacht Club, Glenarvan is disdainful of the English. He is first and foremost a Scot, a nobleman and sailor, devoted to his wife, generous to his servants and relishing adventure, especially when it involved his pride and joy, the ss *Duncan*, his brand new steam yacht. His membership of the Royal Thames Yacht Club was inspired by his wish to compete in sailing in the name of Scotland rather than from any wish to join the snobbish English sailing fraternity. Lady Helena, his wife of three months at the start of the adventure, also a Scot from nearby Kilpatrick, was not from an aristocratic background. Her father William Tuffnel had been an explorer, but she was already an orphan when Glenarvan met her. He recognised her charm, determination and intelligence and at the age of 22 she became Lady Glenarvan and was immediately adored by the household and servants at Malcolm Castle.

The secret of the hammerhead shark!

The plot is full of twists and turns from beginning to end and starts in a curious fashion. On 26 July 1864, Edward Glenarvan was completing the sea trials of his new steam yacht the *Duncan* in the North Channel between Scotland and Ireland. His intended maiden voyage is a honeymoon excursion with Lady Helena to the Mediterranean and especially the Greek islands. More than satisfied with the ship's performance in the Firth of Clyde, Lord Glenarvan gave the order for the *Duncan* to head for home when the captain, John Mangles, noticed a giant fish following in the wake of the yacht. It was identified as being a hammerhead shark and Glenarvan gave the order to capture it, summoning Lady Helena to witness the ugly shark with hammer-like protuberances on its head[1]. In fact, Verne was inaccurate in locating this type of sub-tropical shark so far north up the west coast, but its very ugliness adds drama to the start of the novel. The beast was duly caught by the crew who landed it on the deck and, knowing that the stomachs of voracious sharks often contain surprising items, cut up the beast and were astonished to discover a sealed bottle, which Glenarvan commanded them to remove carefully. The bottle was cleaned and was examined by Lord Glenarvan, Lady Helena, and Major MacNabbs, a cousin of Glenarvan. It was revealed as being a *Veuve Cliquot* champagne bottle! With great care Glenarvan managed to remove the corroded seal and extracted some papers. They had been badly damaged by infiltration of sea water but it was soon established that there were three separate documents, one in English, one in French and a third in German. It further transpired that the contents of the documents were identical and thus that certain words illegible in one

Watched by his wife, Lord Glenarvan carefully withdraws the documents from the bottle.

Riou

language could be interpreted by their presence in one of the other two languages. In this manner, the documents could be partially deciphered and indicated that two years earlier, a ship named the *Britannia* sailed from Glasgow and had sunk at 37 degrees 11 minutes latitude. The longitude was missing and the owner was visible only as 'captain Gr'. The message ended with a desperate plea for help. This use of enigmatic clues became a favourite device of Verne's in several of his novels and, as we will see, reappears in *Mirifiques aventures de Maître Antifer*.

Having achieved this much in the way of interpretation, the *Duncan* was by then entering the Clyde and Captain Mangles asked for instructions. Lord Glenarvan was decisive. Aid must be given to the shipwrecked vessel and accordingly he ordered Mangles to head for Dumbarton, where Lady Helena could disembark for Malcolm Castle, while he would continue to London to report the affair to the admiralty. As they ascended the Clyde, further scrutiny of the papers revealed that the catastrophe appeared to have occurred off the coast of Patagonia and by referring to a shipping gazette it was discovered that the identity of the captain was Captain Grant, a sailor known to Glenarvan, as having set sail for the Pacific in an attempt to found a Scottish colony. The crucial missing element remained the longitude, without which it was impossible to locate the site of the catastrophe.

On reaching Dumbarton, Lady Helena continued by coach to Malcolm Castle while her husband proceeded by express train to London, where he intended to persuade the lords of the admiralty to launch a rescue expedition. Before departing, Glenarvan had telegraphed a notice to *The Times*, the London newspaper, stating that anyone wishing information on the plight of the three-masted ship, the *Britannia* of Glasgow, under the command of Captain Grant, should contact Lord Glenarvan at Malcolm Castle, Luss in the County of Dumbarton, Scotland.

The arrival of Captain Grant's children

Two days later, in the evening, the head manservant announced to Lady Helena that two children had arrived asking to speak to Lord Glenarvan. She requested that they should be shown into her presence and a boy and a girl entered. They had travelled by train from Perth to Balloch and then had walked the eight miles to Castle Malcolm. The girl was 16 and the boy 12 and it was clear that they were physically and emotionally exhausted. It transpired that they were the children of Captain Grant and that purely by coincidence they had seen Lord Glenarvan's notice in *The Times*. Their father, a widower, was a successful sea captain from Dundee who shared Glenarvan's disdain of the English and believed that the future of Scotland required the creation of her own colonies. He had set sail in the *Britannia* in 1861 in search of colonial possibilities in the Pacific islands, but nothing had been heard of him since June 1862. During this time his two children had been lodged with an elderly cousin and when she died, Mary had devoted herself to bringing up her young brother. Gently, Helena spared them the detail of the shipwreck contained in the documents; namely that only her father and two sailors had survived and that they had suffered at the hands of 'Indians'. She assured them that Lord Glenarvan would persuade the admiralty to mount a rescue mission and insisted that they should stay the night at the castle.

In the morning Lord Glenarvan arrived in his coach whereupon the two children threw themselves on him in gratitude. However, he brought bad news, for the admiralty lords had refused to despatch a boat in search of Captain Grant. At this point, an emotional Lady Helena, who had virtually adopted the Grant children as her own, pleaded with her husband to abandon their nuptial voyage to the Mediterranean and instead to mount his own rescue expedition in the *Duncan*. The idea had already occurred to Glenarvan, but he had not expected her to wish to abandon their holiday cruise. The Grant children begged to join the search and the Glenarvans had not the heart to reject their pleadings. Lord Glenarvan ordered his captain John Mangles to sail the *Duncan* immediately to Glasgow to prepare for a voyage that might in fact necessitate a circumnavigation of the globe. Accordingly, Mangles moored at Steamboat Quay and took on food supplies to last for two years. He enlarged the bunkers to load the maximum amount of coal and organised the cabins to accommodate Lord and Lady Glenarvan, Major MacNabbs, the Grant children, Lady Glenarvan's maid, the steward and his wife from Malcolm Castle and a total crew of 25. The *Duncan* was a 210 ton steam yacht with two masts, but its main asset was its high pressure steam engine capable of driving the twin screws to achieve a speed of 17 knots. Once the interior arrangements and loading were completed, the *Duncan* was ready for sailing and the entire complement gathered at Glasgow on 24 August to attend a service of blessing of the

The children of Captain Grant arrive at Malcolm Castle and beg
Lady Glenarvan to help them.
Riou

voyage in St Mungo's cathedral in the company of a vast congregation[2]. At midnight, the boilers were lit and a head of steam had been achieved by the time the tide turned and the *Duncan* set sail on the ebb tide at three in the morning. Under the skilled guidance of Captain Mangles there was no need of a pilot. Within an hour the *Duncan* had reached Dumbarton and by six in the morning had rounded the Mull of Kintyre and sailed through the North Channel to the open Atlantic.

The mystery guest!

At this point in the story, the direct Scottish connection ends, except of course, for the distinctively Scottish characteristics of the protagonists. However, reference must be made to a further character, who progressively becomes crucial to the adventure and at the end of the novel shows his commitment to Scotland and to the Glenarvan household in particular. As the *Duncan* headed west on the Atlantic, a stranger emerged from his cabin and calmly introduced himself. This man was Monsieur Paganel, General Secretary of the *Société de Géographie de Paris*[3]. A tall, thin, bespectacled man, Jacques-Eliacin-François-Marie Paganel was an erudite walking encyclopaedia on all things geographical. He was essentially an 'armchair' geographer with a pedantic book knowledge of the globe, but little personal experience of the real world. To correct this defect he had embarked on a mission to India, but in Glasgow had made a fundamental error. The *Duncan* had been moored next to the *Scotia* and the absent-minded Paganel had boarded the wrong vessel and rather than sailing for the east had joined the *Duncan* on its westwards quest. On discovering his error, it was decided to disembark Paganel at the first opportunity at Madeira where the *Duncan* was due to coal. However, deciding that Madeira had already been the subject of much geographical research and thus held little interest for him, Paganel decided to continue aboard the *Duncan*. Similar pretexts ensued at the Canary Islands and at Cap Verde, and the more Paganel heard about the purpose of the voyage the more intrigued he became and the more he anticipated the experience of travelling in relative terra incognito in Patagonia. In spite of his eccentricities Paganel progressively became a highly-valued member of the expedition, as his book learning is transformed by practical application and he becomes virtually a man of action.

M Paganel, the erudite secretary of the Paris Geographical Society,
demonstrates his eccentricity by boarding the wrong ship at Glasgow.
Riou

The circumnavigation

The real adventure begins when the *Duncan* sails through the Magellan Straits and steams up the coast of Patagonia to Conception on the 37th parallel, the latitude on which the *Britannia* had been shipwrecked according to the message in the bottle. With no sign or word of Captain Grant, Lord Glenarvan leads a party from the crew together with Paganel, MacNabbs and the young boy Robert Grant, to follow the 37th parallel across Patagonia and the Argentinian pampas with many an extraordinary adventure en route. They rejoin the *Duncan* on the Atlantic coast and set sail eastwards following the same parallel of latitude eventually reaching Australia. Here further cruel adventures befall the entire group involving treachery and attempted piracy by a group of convicts in Australia. The leader of the fugitive convicts is no less than Tom Ayrton, the quarter master of the *Britannia* under the command of the missing Captain Grant. Falling out with his captain, Ayrton had attempted to organise a mutiny, but failed to gain the support of the crew. Grant had punished him by landing him on the coast of Western Australia, where eventually he had assumed the leadership of a band of escaped convicts.

Glenarvan and his companions searched fruitlessly for Grant in New South Wales before returning to the coast only to find that the *Duncan* had sailed under false orders given by Ayrton and with him aboard to make good his escape from Australia. Having failed to find Grant in Australia and in the process having fallen victim to piracy, Glenarvan hired a passage aboard a broken down old steamer, the *Macquarie*, headed for Auckland in New Zealand situated once more on 37 degrees latitude. Again, fate took a hand as the crew became drunk and the ship ran aground on the west coast of New Zealand. If this were not catastrophe enough, Glenarvan and his companions were captured and threatened with death by a Maori tribe. Paganel displayed his ingenuity by inventing a subterfuge involving the stimulation of a volcanic eruption from the crater of the tribe's sacred mountain, giving the party an opportunity to escape and trek across New Zealand following faithfully the latitude of 37 degrees. To their amazement, they rediscovered the *Duncan* anchored precisely at this latitude on the east coast. Amid scenes of joy, Glenarvan was reunited with Lady Helena and Robert with his sister Mary.

The rescuers are warmly welcomed back at Malcolm Castle
after their global adventure.
Riou

Once aboard the *Duncan*, Ayrton was interrogated by Glenarvan and a deal was struck. Ayrton agreed to tell all he knew about the *Britannia* and in return would be abandoned on an island rather than face trial in Britain. Consulting a map, Paganel indicated that by continuing their course along the 37th parallel, they would intercept Tabor Island where Ayrton could be marooned. However, on approaching the island, fires were seen and a voice was heard that the Grant children recognised as being their father's. A joyful reunion ensued and the mystery of the loss of the *Britannia* was resolved. Ayrton was left to his fate and the *Duncan* headed for her home port of Dumbarton and a hearty welcome at Castle Malcolm. It had not escaped the attention of the company that the relationship between Mary Grant and Captain Mangles had become increasingly warm throughout the long adventure. Sure enough, the pair were married in Glasgow Cathedral two weeks later by the same minister who had wished the *Duncan* godspeed nine months earlier. The novel ends on a farcical note when amidst all the celebrations it becomes clear that Paganel, by now established as a hero rather than an eccentric, and who has contributed greatly to the success of the expedition, admires a cousin of MacNabbs, Miss Arabella. Paganel confides his affection for her to MacNabbs but claims that he is unworthy of her and cannot propose marriage. After much persuasion he reveals in confidence the reason to MacNabbs. While captured by the Maoris he had been tattooed all over his body! He is persuaded that this is no impediment and Arabella and Paganel are married in the chapel of Malcolm Castle amidst great rejoicing.

The epic adventure thus ends in a state of delirium. Above all, Captain Grant had been rescued and had become a national hero, who was still determined to search for a Scottish colony overseas. His daughter Mary had developed into a young woman and had married with much pomp in Glasgow's famous cathedral. Robert, mature beyond his years, was determined to become a mariner like his father. Paganel too has married, and to a Scottish lass. Meanwhile, Lord and Lady Glenarvan can resume their interrupted married bliss, surrounded by their devoted servants at Malcolm Castle and no longer surrogate parents to the Grant children.

The Children of Captain Grant is perhaps the best-known of Verne's Scottish novels worldwide, and with 40,000 copies printed it had the largest print run. It reveals his almost uncritical admiration of the Scots. Certain features are especially indicative of this sentiment. In his immense

The transformation of Paganel from pedantic scholar and bachelor
to husband and honorary Scot.
Riou

output of *Voyages Extraordinaires* novels, female characters developed in depth are quite sparse and yet in this novel we find not one, but two heroines. Lady Helena typifies the qualities in Verne's mind of the wife of a Scottish aristocrat. She is determined and decisive and fears for nothing other than the safety of those around her, but at the same time is gentle and compassionate. At the beginning of the tale Mary Grant is a responsible girl who has devoted her young life to the upbringing of her brother, but beneath the surface she is deeply emotional and is desperate to find her adored father. A bond rapidly develops between the two women and some of the scenes involving them are both tender and moving. After the rescue of her father, Mary is freed of the responsibility of looking after her brother and almost unconsciously has achieved womanhood and can become a loving wife to John Mangles.

The male characters, with the obvious exception of the villainous Ayrton, share in common the virtues that Verne attributes to Scotsmen, and there is not a hint of criticism nor any blemish on their character. They are portrayed as having moral and physical courage in abundance and are steadfast in their loyalty. They share a love of the sea and under the tutelage of John Mangles, the emergence of Robert Grant as an aspiring mariner testifies to Verne's belief that the salt of the sea runs in the veins of the true Scot. The theme of transformation is equally evident in the case of the non-Scot. Leaving Glasgow in the *Duncan* as a myopic scholar given to pedantry, by the end of the book Paganel has become a man of adventure, has turned his book learning to practical advantage and has forsaken his confirmed bachelor existence in favour of marriage. In effect he has become an honorary Scot in Verne's eyes[4]!

Verne's experience of Scotland when he wrote the manuscript was limited to less than a week. He had visited the quays of Glasgow Harbour, and on the train to Balloch had seen glimpses of the canalised River Clyde. He had spent a matter of minutes at the pier of Luss en route by steamer to Inversnaid. From these fragmentary and rapid glimpses, he established locales to launch his novel into realms that only existed from his research and in his imagination to produce a tour de force and a 'geographical' novel par excellence, but from which the Scottish dimension is never absent in one form or another.

The first two novels considered so far have certain characteristics in common. Both involve travel by ship within a defined geographical space and both involve the upper echelons of Scottish society. The contrast with the next story could not be stronger. *The Underground City* is not only on land but largely subterranean and the characters portrayed are almost all working class.

Notes

1   According to the National Maritime Museum in Plymouth, there are no records of hammerhead shark, a semi-tropical fish, having been sighted north of the south of Wales. Other species of shark can be seen in the Firth of Clyde, but with the hammerhead (*Zygaena malleus*) Verne made a choice justified by its macabre features rather than biological likelihood.

2   As in *The Blockade Runners*, Verne situates an episode in St Mungo's cathedral even though he had never seen the interior.

3   With his first hand knowledge of *La Société de Géographie de Paris*, Verne may have had a particular General Secretary in mind as the model for Paganel. There has been much amused speculation as to who this might have been!

4   Flushed with the acclaim and financial success of a stage production of *Around the World in Eighty Days*, Verne collaborated on the staging of *The Children of Captain Grant*. The plot was drastically changed and the play was a critical failure.

CHAPTER SIX

The Underground City

BY THE TIME VERNE picked up his pen to write another Scottish novel 12 years had elapsed since the publication of *The Children of Captain Grant*. Moreover, in the interval he had published two of his most successful and remunerative novels, *Twenty Thousand Leagues under the Sea* and *Around the World in Eighty Days*. One may wonder why he returned to a Scottish theme. In fact, as well as his compulsive desire to write on a daily basis, Verne was locked into a demanding series of contracts with Hetzel that required him to produce two to three volumes per annum. We can be sure that Verne still had notes relating to his 1859 journey and that the temptation was strong to exploit a setting dear to his heart, but which he had not so far exploited in a novel – Edinburgh and The Trossachs. Not only did the location differ from that of *The Children of Captain Grant*, but the entire character of the novel is different. Whereas *The Children of Captain Grant* was a series of adventures set in exotic lands, *The Underground City* is almost a *roman noir* and, as opposed to the former novel, which was based on geographical fact assiduously researched by Verne, it is a tale of imagination in which geographical and geological accuracy is partly abandoned in favour of fantasy. Nevertheless, practically all of the setting had been seen by Verne and had had a profound effect on him. In fact, we must imagine that Verne had been turning over in his mind how to exploit his experience of The Trossachs in the form of a novel.

Les Indes noires was published in 1877, when Verne was arguably at the height of his creative powers. At 36,000 copies, the print run was almost as great as *The Children of Captain Grant*. Unlike his long distance novels the majority of the action in *Les Indes noires* takes place within a fifty mile radius, with Loch Katrine as the epicentre. *Les Indes noires* is one of the most translated of Verne's novels with titles in English such as *The Black Indies*, *The Child of the Cavern* and *The Underground City*[1]. It is a complex novel in the sense that here we find, underlying Verne's habitual action-driven plot, ideas on political and social organisation that are implicit rather than explicitly stated. The title refers to the wealth of Britain's coal resources as being equivalent to the perceived riches of India, the jewel in the imperial crown. In contrast to this rather experimental sortie into political ideas, the novel also draws heavily on the atmosphere of the Romantic movement, and specifically the novels of Walter Scott and his narrative poem *The Lady of the Lake*. The supernatural and the use of fear as a literary device create an aura of suspense and impending tragedy, and yet, as with the other Scottish novels discussed thus far, a wedding provides a happy ending.

Two mysterious letters

The story begins as a mystery when a certain James Starr receives a letter at his home in Edinburgh inviting him to travel to the Aberfoyle coalfield the following day where he will find something of great interest[2]. The letter concludes by stating that Starr will be awaited all day at Callander railway station by Harry Ford, son of the former foreman, Simon Ford. We learn that James Starr is an engineer who comes from a solid professional Edinburgh family and is widely respected in the city as a member of several learned societies. He is a sprightly 55-year-old who had spent his professional life as general manager of the Aberfoyle coal mines which had closed a decade previously, being considered as having exhausted their seams. Starr ponders the cryptic letter and his curiosity leads him to decide to go to Callander the following morning. Having made his decision the evening mail delivers a second letter which states that his visit is unnecessary and irrelevant. This letter, delivered at 6pm, is the third delivery of

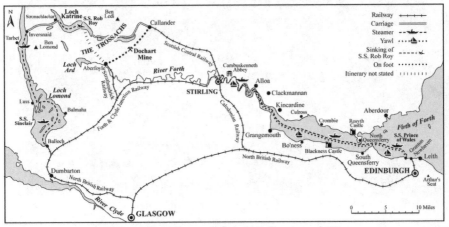

FIG. 8 The itinerary of the *Underground City*

James Starr peruses a mysterious letter from Simon Ford.

J Férat

the day. At this time, as many as five postal deliveries a day were common-place in Edinburgh. The writing is crude and on a rough piece of paper. Clearly it is from a different author and is an unveiled attempt to make him abandon his journey. The effect is the exact opposite of the intention, for Starr becomes all the more determined to get to the bottom of the mystery. [FIG. 8]

Accordingly, early the next morning Starr leaves his house in the Canongate and in rainy weather walks briskly to the General Railway Station and catches the train to Newhaven. From here he makes his way the short distance to Granton Pier to catch the steamer to Stirling. In effect Verne bases the story at this stage on his own 1859 steamer journey which had been undertaken in atrocious weather and he retains the same name of the steamer, the *Prince of Wales*. In fact Starr could easily have travelled to Callander by train in more comfort and more rapidly. Verne 'recycles' some of the description of the Forth estuary included in *Backwards to Britain*, but rather than disembarking at Crombie Point, Starr continues to Stirling where he lands at the Steamboat Quay and walks the five minutes to the railway station and takes the train to Callander[3]. Waiting for him is Harry Ford, son of the old manager of Dochart Pit, Aberfoyle[4]. At this point Verne includes a lengthy treatise on the geological origin of coal and its importance in the British economy. It is a curious passage, of dubious scientific quality and disrupts the continuity of the text. We must assume that he had thoroughly researched this topic, as the text even includes coal production statistics, and was determined to exploit his notes. It is ironic that after this weighty discourse on the origin and distribution of coal, he proceeds to locate the coalfield in question near Aberfoyle where the existence of coal is a geological impossibility!

Starr and Harry Ford walk the four miles to the Yarrow shaft of the Dochart mine, both the distance and weather conditions recalling Verne's own walk from Crombie Point with the Reverend William Smith to Oakley Castle in 1859[5]. As the mine is approached, the pair pass through derelict and overgrown mine works, pitheads and abandoned railway lines, rendering James Starr both nostalgic and depressed. An hour after leaving Callander they reach the Yarrow shaft and via a series of ladders descend deep underground. Reaching the bottom of the shaft, they follow a gallery when suddenly a boulder comes crashing down near them – the first of an increasing number of menacing events.

In *The Underground City,* James Starr arrived at Stirling's Steamboat Quay from Edinburgh. In this photograph the *Edinburgh Castle* steamer prepares to depart from Stirling for the return sail to Edinburgh.

Stirling County Library and Archives Service

A *happy reunion*

Eventually Starr and Harry Ford enter a more open area, partially lit by a ventilation shaft, where the Ford family has its home in a kind of troglodyte dwelling. Here Harry's parents, Simon and Madge, are anxiously awaiting their visitor's arrival and a warm reunion of the old friends takes place. Sixty-five years old, Simon Ford had been the foreman of the Dochart mine, the most important in the Aberfoyle coalfield, and when it closed had decided to continue to live underground where he had spent all his working life. Starr and Ford had the deepest respect and admiration for each other and when the mine closed both were heartbroken. In the case of Simon Ford, his decision to live underground was due to his obsession to hunt on a daily basis for possible new seams which could bring the mine back to life. It is this context that led Ford to contact Starr, but he refuses to reveal his secret until their guest has had a hearty lunch. Not for the first time Verne recites what he considers to be a typical Scottish menu of homely but nourishing food. A 'hotch-potch' of meat soup is followed by cock-a-leekie chicken and leek ragout.

Harry Ford, a young man of few words but resolute, loyal and devoted
to his family and friends.

J Férat

In turn a haggis is produced and then dessert consists of cheese and oat cakes[6]. The whole meal is washed down with the best Edinburgh ale and rounded off by a 25-year-old whisky. When the meal is accomplished, Starr shows Simon Ford the second letter that he has received. None of the family can recognise the handwriting and the mystery remains. Simon Ford is now ready to reveal the reason why he has invited his old boss and the three men leave the cottage[7].

The secret revealed

Simon leads the two others along a series of galleries until they reach the face of the last coal seam, where he himself had dug the very last lump of coal. Here, the day before, he had detected firedamp, a sure indication of the existence of coal. Examining the wall he was astonished to discover that the cracks from which the gas had been escaping had been newly filled in. Throughout their explorations of the mine the father and son had experienced strange noises, flashes of light and fallen rocks as if some unknown presence was attempting to make them abandon their hunt for coal. Undeterred, Harry climbed on his father's shoulders and picked away to unblock the cracks. Immediately, firedamp began to escape again and amid jubilation, for the existence of coal was proven, the three men returned to join Madge at the cottage. The following day they return to the site, taking Madge with them, and James Starr prepares to dynamite the rock wall. The explosion creates a large hole and Harry clambers through to discover a vast cavern. He calls the others to follow him and for an hour they explore this immense space, Harry leading the way with his lamp. Suddenly, there is a noise like a beating of huge wings and Harry's lamp falls from his hand and smashes, plunging them into darkness. Is this the latest episode in the mysterious series of inexplicable events? They grope their way for several miles towards the hole that Starr had dynamited, only to find that it has been closed up and they are imprisoned!

The rescue

At this point Verne introduces a plot within a plot which in fact is something of a diversion from the main story. A friend of Harry's, Jack Ryan, a jovial young man adept at traditional Scottish singing and dancing, had

Simon Ford whose persistence leads to the discovery of vast coal reserves and to the creation of the underground city.

J Férat

Jack Ryan is a unique creation in Verne's Scottish stories. He is full of fun,
song and dance but plays a crucial role in the underground rescue.

J Férat

moved to Ayrshire at the closure of Aberfoyle coalfield and worked on a farm. He had visited Harry on the day of James Starr's arrival and had invited his friend to the clan festival at Irvine in Ayrshire eight days later. Irvine is dominated by Dundonald Castle and on the night of the festival strange flames are emitted from the castle tower. Mistaking the flames for the harbour light on a dark and stormy night, a Norwegian brig crashes into the rocks at the foot of the cliff. But for the heroic rescue efforts of Jack Ryan and his friends the crew would certainly have perished. Recovered from the rescue effort, Jack Ryan becomes concerned at the absence of Harry Ford, who had promised to attend the festival. This state of anxiety is shared with respect to James Starr by a number of Edinburgh worthies, including the Lord Provost and the President of the Royal Institution. They had discovered from his maid that Starr had set off for Granton Pier to catch the *Prince of Wales* steamer but nothing else is known of his bizarre absence. Accordingly, a message is published in the main newspapers and posted at railway stations asking for any information of his whereabouts to be transmitted urgently to the President of the Royal Institution. Meanwhile, Jack Ryan decides to take the train to Callander and search for his friend. At Irvine station he catches sight of the President's notice. On arrival at Callander he hastens to the Dochart pit. Ominously, when he descends the shaft, one of the ladders close to the bottom has been burned and Jack is unable to proceed to the Ford's cottage. By now thoroughly alarmed, Jack Ryan recalls the notice he saw at Irvine station. He hurries back to Callander and catches the first train to Edinburgh and rushes to the Royal Institution where the President immediately mounts a search party. The Royal Institution on Princes Street, now occupied by the National Gallery of Scotland, housed a number of scientific and artistic organisations including The Royal Society of Edinburgh, Scotland's leading institution in these fields.

With the help of a rope ladder the party reaches the bottom of the shaft and hastens to Ford's cottage only to find it deserted. Jack Ryan spots a faint glow in a tunnel which seems to be inviting them to follow. Indeed, this mysterious light guides them along a series of tunnels until it disappears at an opening in the rock. Scrambling through they confront the terrifying sight of four bodies stretched out on the floor. It is Madge, Harry and Simon Ford and James Starr, whether dead or alive is uncertain. As they approach, Madge raises her head and the others are soon revived by drinking drops of a strong cordial. They had survived for ten days because a loaf of bread and a jug of water had mysteriously appeared three times. To the previous threatening gestures of an unknown adversary were now to be added the life saving actions of someone who had guided the rescue party and had also provided some sustenance to the survivors.

Coal City is born

After the success of the rescue, Verne now moves the clock forward three years. The extent of the newly-discovered coal seams is enormous, extending from the Ayrshire coast at Irvine, under Loch Katrine and as far north as the Caledonian Canal. In this New Aberfoyle coalfield pride of place is occupied by Coal City, a new town built on the banks of a lagoon, Lake Malcolm, within the huge cavern. The whole town is powered by electricity including huge disks in the roof of the cavern which simulate sunlight. It is linked to the surface by a double track railway, which not only serves the needs of the mine and its inhabitants, but also allows tourists to visit this remarkable site. The Fords move from their cottage into Coal City where they are joined by Jack Ryan. Verne paints a picture of an utopian society, living in comfort and harmony, untroubled by the Scottish weather and in a spirit of optimism believing that one day Coal City could rival the national capital Edinburgh. In Verne's words:

> The population, having the same interests, the same tastes and more or less the same income, constituted to all intents and purposes one large family. They knew one other, mixed with one another, and the need to go and look for pleasures above ground was seldom felt (Chapter 13)[8].

How far this idyllic portrayal diverged from the real horror of life in the 19th century Scottish mining industry can easily be imagined!

The discovery of the 'Child of the Cavern'

One Sunday Harry Ford and his friend Jack Ryan are taking a stroll along the shore of Loch Malcolm. A bigger contrast between their two moods cannot be possible, for Jack is his usual irrepressible self while Harry is deep in gloomy thought. In fact, since the strange events which

The rescue party discovers with horror the four victims collapsed
unconscious on the floor.
J Férat

Crowds gather on Sundays on the shore of Lake Malcolm to enjoy
dancing led by the pipes of Jack Ryan.

J Férat

led to the discovery of new coal seams, Harry has become obsessed with finding an explanation for the dangers and threats which almost killed his family. The romantic Jack attributes the mysteries to goblins, but the hard-headed Harry is convinced that there is a rational explanation and that possibly a madman is intent on destroying the mine and its occupants. At the same time, some kind-hearted being sustained the life of the trapped Ford family and James Starr. This contradiction between good and evil disturbs Harry and he confides in Jack that he has explored the deepest shaft of the mine and has encountered a flapping of wings and is convinced that he heard groans. The conversation is concluded by the pair agreeing to explore this shaft together on the morrow.

As planned, the two friends duly set off accompanied by three miners and reach the mouth of the shaft. Harry is lowered down on a rope 200 feet long and on reaching the bottom his groping hands touch what undoubtedly is a body. Swinging round his lamp Harry discovers to his amazement that the body is that of a live but unconscious girl. Speed is essential to get the child into the care of Madge. Clasping her to his chest, Harry tugs on the rope as a signal that he is to be hauled back up the shaft. All goes well at first but then Harry is attacked by a huge and vicious bird. Attempting to drive it off with his knife, he inadvertently slices halfway through the rope and as the strands fray he and the girl are in danger of falling back to the bottom of the shaft to join the wounded bird. Just before the rope snaps, Harry grasps it above the fray and, at the end of his strength, is finally pulled out of the shaft still clutching the child.

After the horror and darkness of the story thus far, Verne now introduces a gentle and tender touch. The young girl is revealed not as a child, but as a young woman of 16 who gives her name as Nell. She is desperately weak, but gradually responds to Madge's nourishment and gentle tending. She speaks the same Gaelic language as the Fords but any questioning of her background throws her into a state of terror and silence. Rapidly she becomes Madge's right hand, delighting in helping her with the housework. The Ford family quickly come to love her, none more so than Harry. His admiration becomes even more intense when in conversation it emerges that she was the angel who had brought food to the imprisoned group and who had guided the rescuers to them. Harry regales her with accounts of the outside world at the surface

Harry discovers the unconscious body of Nell, the 'Child of the Cavern'.
J Férat

Harry is attacked by a giant owl and accidentally slices his rescue rope.
J Férat

which she is impatient to see once her eyes become accustomed to stronger light.

Nell sees the outside world for the first time

Nell's eyes gradually strengthen as they become accustomed to the electric light which illuminates Coal City, and a month after her discovery the moment is ripe for her to see natural daylight. It is arranged that Harry, who by now is deeply in love with Nell, but will not propose to her until she has seen both him and the outside world in daylight, will take Nell above ground accompanied by Starr and Jack Ryan. A two day trip is planned and at nine o'clock in the evening, chosen to protect Nell's eyes, the group take the last train up to the surface. At New Aberfoyle station they take the train on the branch line which joins the Forth and Clyde Junction Railway to Stirling[9]. From here they walk the short distance to the banks of the Forth where a small sailboat, hired by James Starr, awaits them. Nell marvels at the heaven full of stars and the rising moon, but lulled by the movement of the boat she falls asleep on Harry's shoulder. Two hours later the little boat reaches Granton Pier and Nell awakes. Verne is now back on familiar ground, his beloved Edinburgh, and the narrative reflects his own experience in 1859. The party walk from Leith, past Calton Hill and climb up to the Canongate and Holyrood Palace. They continue their climb over Salisbury Crags until they reach the summit of Arthur's Seat where they sit down to watch the sunrise. James Starr quotes Walter Scott's opinion of the view from Arthur's Seat expressed in *The Heart of Midlothian*:

> If I were to choose a spot from which the rising or setting sun could be seen to the greatest possible advantage, it would be that.

As the first rays of the sun protrude above the horizon, Verne produces one of his most moving passages as one by one the facets of the landscapes are revealed to Nell, culminating in her exclamation on bended knees 'God, how beautiful your world is!' as she faints in Harry's arms.

Verne's reminiscence of his 1859 journey continues as the group repair to Lambré's Hotel for breakfast before taking the train to Glasgow and passing the night at Comrie's Royal Hotel on George Square. So end a night and day which stretch credulity somewhat in that they required

Madge Ford, devoted wife and mother and protector of the orphan Nell.
J Férat

the frail Nell to travel overnight from Aberfoyle to Edinburgh with just two hours sleep before traversing the full width of the city on foot and climbing Arthur's Seat and descending to Princes Street before taking the train to Glasgow! The following day, the travellers catch the train to Balloch where they board the *Sinclair*, an excursion steamer bound for the head of Loch Lomond. Here Verne gives an ecstatic account of the landscape and history of the loch as interpreted by James Starr to Nell. The poetic nature of this description, recalled from his 1859 visit, leaves us in no doubt that Verne himself ached to revisit this fairyland which, as we have seen, he accomplished two years after the publication of *Les Indes noires*. The companions disembark at Inversnaid pier, take lunch at the hotel and stroll the few yards to view the magnificent waterfall. As they continue their journey by coach, James Starr changes the theme of his description to Nell to the adventures of Rob Roy, the name of the little boat bobbing in Loch Katrine waiting to take them to the Trossachs pier. Jack Ryan captures the magical mood of Loch Katrine by singing a traditional song accompanied by a Highland bagpiper in the stern of the boat[10].

I

'Beautiful lochs with sleepy waters,
Can I never see again
Your charming shores,
Beautiful lochs of Scotland
On your banks I found the traces,
Of your lamented heroes,
I recognised their noble races,
And Walter Scott about them sang!
I saw the tower where
witches
Prepared their frugal meal.
And the vast moors of
heather,
Where Fingal's shadow
returns.

II

I saw there one dark night
The mad dance of goblins.
While in the shadow appeared
The face of old Puritans!
And amongst the wild rocks,
In the evening I thought I surprised
again,
Waverley leading Flora MacIvor
Towards your shores!

III

The Lady of the Lake doubtless
Arrives,
Straying alone on her palfrey,
And the brave Diana listens
To the echo of Rob Roy's horn!
It seems to me that here Fergus
In times of yore,
Fergus had been heard amongst
his clans,
Playing his warrior pibrochs and
Roused the echo of the
Highlands.

IV

However far from you, poetic lochs,
Destiny leads my steps,
Ravines, rocks, ancient caves,
My eyes will not forget you!
O vision too soon ended,
Can you not come back to me!
Here is to you, old Caledonia,
Here is to you, my best memory!
Beautiful lochs of Scotland!'

By now Nell is overwhelmed by the emotions of the last two days and
Harry asks her gently if she would wish to live permanently above ground.

Nell shakes her head and declares that she could not bear to leave the simple life underground. In that case Harry asks tenderly, would she give him her hand in marriage? Nell quietly gives her assent, but before she can complete her sentence, the *Rob Roy* comes to a juddering halt as her keel strikes the bottom of the loch. The explanation is soon evident. It appears as if an enormous crack has opened draining the waters of the loch. James Starr quickly realises that New Aberfoyle must be inundated and Coal City threatened with extinction[11].

The final drama

Fortunately, the vast cavern and its dense network of tunnels absorb the deluge and no lives are lost. The water of Loch Katrine rapidly drains away and the only permanent effect is raising the level of Loch Malcolm by a few feet. Harry's parents are safe and sound and their cottage undamaged. The catastrophe is generally attributed to a natural geological fault but James Starr and the Fords are less sanguine. Was this again the work of the malevolent spirit which had left them in peace for the last three years? The three men explore the pillars which had supported the cavern's roof and sure enough find traces of a deliberate explosion. James Starr comes to the conclusion that whatever human hand was responsible for the collapse and all the previous unexplained events, it must be someone like themselves with an intimate knowledge of the mine.

Nell, still silent on her origins, is spared this opinion, for the three men sense that she knows more than she is prepared to divulge. Accordingly, the marriage is arranged for a month hence, with James Starr agreeing to give Nell away. As if this news has enraged the unknown spirit, a series of dangerous episodes follow one on the heels of another. A fire breaks out in a gallery which is clearly due to arson. Another gallery collapses due to the sawing through of the pit props and Harry himself is threatened when the tramway on which he is travelling is derailed by a log placed on the rails. It seems clear that Harry himself is the target of these attacks and that his impending marriage has precipitated this new danger. A week before the planned wedding, Nell leaves the cottage early in the morning. She utters an appalling cry which brings the whole household running to her help. The cause of her alarm is soon apparent. Pinned to the door is a note which states;

Simon Ford, you have stolen the last seam of our old mines from
me! Harry, your son, has stolen Nell from me! Woe betide you!
Woe betide you all! Woe betide New Aberfoyle!

The note is signed 'Silfax'.

James Starr at once recognises the handwriting as being the same as that
of the second letter attempting to dissuade him from coming to Aberfoyle.

Nell is utterly distressed and Starr turns to Simon Ford to demand to
know the identity of this person who signs himself 'Silfax'. Simon Ford
knows him only too well. He was the old 'penitent', the name given to the
person who crept along the floors of mine galleries exploding pockets of
firedamp in the days before the invention of the Davy Lamp. Silfax was
memorable for his use of a giant snowy owl[12] which would fly up with a
lighted wick to areas of the roof that Silfax could not reach. At the closure
of the mine he had disappeared with a young orphan child and he was
generally regarded as deranged caused by the danger of his job. At this
point, Nell, who has been comforted by Madge speaks up. She is the
child looked after by Silfax, who in fact is her great-grandfather. He too
had discovered the existence of new coal seams, but in his mad state was
determined that none should share his secret. She had lived with him and
his giant owl in the recesses of the Dochart pit until the Fords had made
their sensational discovery. All the strange happenings could now be
explained as being the work of Silfax, aided by the owl, as he tried to prevent the reopening of the mine. His fury was intensified by the impending
marriage of Nell to Harry, for he regarded the Fords, who like him had
decided to remain resident in the mine, as his enemies – hence the vitriolic
note pinned to their cottage door.

In spite of the threat, no further incidents occur during the preparations
for the marriage. The entire population of Coal City congregates at St
Giles' chapel on the shores of Loch Malcolm and after Harry has pronounced his vows and Nell is about to respond with hers, a massive rock
suddenly detaches itself from the cavern releasing firedamp gas which
rises up to the roof. Immediately afterwards, a small boat is thrust out
into the loch and standing up in it is a bearded old man accompanied by
the giant owl. He cries out 'the firedamp! Woe betide you all'. Sizing up
the danger, Jack Ryan dives into the loch and begins swimming towards
Silfax who, seeing his approach, takes the lighted wick from his lamp and
commands the owl to fly up to the accumulation of gas. Within seconds

The climax of the action. The demented Silfax attempts to destroy
the underground city by collapsing the cavern roof.

J Férat

New Aberfoyle would have been destroyed by the explosion and the collapse of the cavern roof, had Nell not cried out to the owl to come to her. It drops the wick into the lake and glides down to Nell's feet. Frustrated by this action old Silfax leaps into the lake and neither Jack nor Harry can rescue him from the dark waters. Six months later, the disrupted wedding ceremony is recommenced. As for the owl, a few days after the death of Silfax it disappears, seeming to resent Harry in particular. So the tale ends on a happy note, but from time to time, the owl is seen gliding eerily over the surface of Loch Malcolm as a reminder of the past menace.

A *novel of contradictions*

Les Indes noires has attracted more literary interest than many of Verne's novels. In some ways there are imperfections and inconsistencies, especially in terms of the chronology of events. We know that this is one novel where the hand of the publisher Hetzel weighed heavily. Two chapters were excised, the ending was changed and many of Verne's ideas, especially the notion of Britain becoming an underground nation and society, were rejected, to the extent that Verne claimed that he hardly recognised his manuscript. It nevertheless remains one of Verne's most powerful novels in terms of plot, characterisation, atmosphere, and with one exception, the authenticity of the Scottish setting. The exception is the inaccuracy of the geological setting. In locating his coalfield near Aberfoyle he chose a geologically impossible site. It is intriguing to speculate why Verne, who had seen active coal mining in western Fife, should have chosen to situate the action at the foot of the Trossachs. This poser may be easily answered since he required specific qualities of landscape and atmosphere for his tale. He needed a landscape of mystery and threat, where the existence of supernatural beings was credible. Moreover, he needed a large loch, which after shattering earth movements would convulsively drain into the mine. The Trossachs, which Verne found enchanting in terms of beauty, while echoing the armed struggle between Rob Roy MacGregor and the Duke of Montrose, and whose atmosphere was redolent of the supernatural, suited the plot ideally. Shortage of time had denied Verne the opportunity to view a Scottish mine at Oakley in 1859 and his manifest knowledge of mining technology stemmed from reading and from a visit to the mine of Anzin in northern France[13].

The strength of the characterisation stems from the fact that in a story which draws heavily on mysterious and possibly supernatural incidents, the dramatis personae consists of people who are solid and tenacious, but with a profound underlying kindness; qualities which Verne considers as typifying the Scots. The former manager of the mine, James Starr, is portrayed as a highly esteemed model of the middle classes. He is a distinguished engineer, well-connected in Edinburgh's bourgeois community, but without arrogance and dedicated to the wellbeing of society at large, including its less privileged members. Simon Ford and his son Harry are portrayed as being physically and morally strong, doers rather than dreamers and fiercely loyal to the only way of life that they know: that of the miner. Madge is seen to be calm, practical and warm-hearted and a fierce guardian of harmony in the Ford household. Her 'adoption' of Nell suggests a love for a daughter that she never had herself. In contrast to these solid, well-defined characters, Jack Ryan is portrayed as a fey young man, full of humour, believing in fairies and goblins and always looking for an excuse to burst into a traditional song. He is a perfect counterpoint to the rather dour and dogged Harry, but is capable of action as his role in the rescue shows. Nell is shown as being timid, overwhelmed by events, but intelligent and determined. Verne shows in her a half child, half young woman, whose future development can only be guessed at, but whose devotion to Harry and his parents is unconfined. Finally, Silfax is the villain of the piece, a surrogate for the supernatural, but whose villainy can be excused in part by his demented state. His obvious care for Nell and the devotion that he shares with the Fords to Old Aberfoyle are his redeeming features. We must not overlook the snowy owl, which after intermittent fleeting appearances in defence of Nell plays a crucial role in the climax of the plot.

The success of *Les Indes noires* may be attributed to its multifaceted character. The book can be interpreted, more or less validly, in so many different ways. Superficially it may resemble a thriller in which, as the plot unfolds, the atmosphere of menace and fear builds up to a crescendo. At a less superficial level, it can be regarded as a romance in which many manifestations of love are evident; the love of Madge for her family, the affection between the Fords and James Starr, the nostalgia for the fondly remembered olden days of a strong mining community, the love of life, music and song on the part of Jack Ryan, the romantic love between

Harry and Nell and underlying all this, Verne's own admiration of Scotland and the Scots. At the level of literary criticism, the novel may be regarded as being allegorical and especially an interplay of opposites. Within the vast 'womb' of the cavern, people live much of their lives in semi-darkness, in a constant temperature, protected from the outside world and nourished with coal by their geological mother. The story is a tale of opposites, of dark and light, day and night, good and evil, love and hate, rational and supernatural.

Yet another dimension is that of social and political commentary. Verne poses the possibility of an alternative lifestyle, a subterranean utopian existence lived by people working for a common cause, in a relatively classless society. In this sense, the novel is unrealistic. Verne lacks reference to the existence in 19th century Scottish mines of child and female labour, a horrific accident rate and incidence of chronic ill-health and illiteracy. The back-breaking and dangerous work and the poverty-stricken existence, are suppressed in favour of an image of contented family life, a strong work ethic and a coherent non-radical society. Verne was surely aware of the socio-political implications of his novel, and the editorial hand of Hetzel restrained his wilder imaginations, but the result is a novel which lacks the social realism of Zola's *Germinal* in favour of a novel deep in local colour, sensitive characterisation, a rapid-action plot and a happy ending which still leaves certain questions unanswered, hanging in the air just like the snowy owl.

Notes

1   The most recent and authentic translation of *Les Indes noires* is *The Underground City*, Luath Press, Edinburgh, 2005, translated by Sarah Crozier. The most recent edition of Scott's *Lady of the Lake* has been published by The Association for Scottish Literary Studies, Glasgow, 2010.

2   The siting of a coalfield near Aberfoyle is a geological impossibility. The nearest coal mines were situated to the east of Stirling at Polmaise. Although Aberfoyle had no coal, there is nevertheless a history of slate quarrying on the mountain behind the village which was sufficiently important for an inclined plane tramway to be built linking the quarries to the railway in 1882, well after Verne's visit.

3   The Steamboat Quay at Stirling was a small wharf on the left bank of the Forth. It no longer exists, but the site is now a small pleasure garden on Shore Road. Verne's description of James Starr walking from the quay to the railway station in five minutes is exactly accurate.

4   If the location of the Aberfoyle coalfield is anomalous, the place names correspond to real localities. The Dochart mine takes its name from Glen Dochart, some ten miles to the north of Loch Katrine and the Yarrow coal seam probably takes its name from the village of Yarrow near Selkirk, in the heart of the Walter Scott country and where Scott attended church.

5   The four mile walk from Callander would place the mine well to the north east of Aberfoyle in an area almost devoid of significant settlement.

6   Verne makes reference to Burns' address to the haggis which he considers as his best ode.

7   Verne terms the Ford's underground house as a 'cottage'. He uses this term rather indiscriminately since in *The Green Ray* he also refers to Helena Campbell's country mansion as a cottage, indicating Verne's lack of comprehension of the English language.

8   Verne's almost idyllic picture of the underground mining community is wildly at odds with the reality of life in Scottish mining communities in the 19th century. An almost feudal system existed in which women and children were exploited just as much as the men. See King, L, *Sair, Sair Wark. Women and Mining in Scotland*, 2001, Kelty.

    The Parliamentary Commission Report into children's employment in Scottish mines makes harrowing reading as the following extracts show;

> Mary McLean. Aged 12 years old; has only wrought three years below, as was off work with crushed legs 12 months.

> William McLean. Aged 12 years old, hewer and putter. Been 18 months below. Works 10 and 12 hours below, not been to any school for three years.

> Janet Allen, eight years old. Works in the pit with sisters Christy and Agnes, done so nine months.

The situation was equally bad for women, viz

> Catherine Kerrr [*sic*], Aged 35, putter (ie pushes the loaded coal tubs), has four children, youngest is seven months old, went below after its birth; obliged to work as husband is short of breath.

9 This branch line, The Strathendrick and Aberfoyle Railway, was not opened until 1882 and so Verne must have anticipated its construction or simply invented it.

10 In fact the song is an amended version of a Verne poem set to music by his friend from his 1859 visit to Loch Katrine, Aristide Hignard. The version translated here is that of the Verne original, as published under its original title of *Souvenirs d'Ecosse*, in Jules Verne. *Textes oubliés*, 1849–1903, Paris, 1979.

11 Verne gives no indication of how the group travelled from the marooned *Rob Roy* to New Aberfoyle, a long and arduous journey over the Duke's Pass.

12 The Snowy Owl (*Nyctea Scandiaca*) is a bird of the sub-arctic tundra very rarely appearing as a vagrant in the far north of Scotland and the Outer Hebrides. Verne's choice is ornithologically dubious but the choice fits the role in that it is a very large and aggressive bird which will attack humans when disturbed. Moreover, by choosing an owl rather than any other raptor, he selected a nocturnal bird with acute night vision and therefore a credible bird to be found in the semi-darkness underground. It is possible that the device of using an owl in his plot derived from his reading of Nodier who describes two incidents involving large birds in The Trossachs, in *Promenade de Dieppe aux montagnes de l'Ecosse*, Paris, Barba, 1821. Firstly, he is pursued aggressively by a 'great white bird' for five or six miles. Secondly, as night falls, Nodier is terrified by a giant owl suddenly springing up from a tree beside him with its prey in its talons. Coincidentally, the magnificent Stewart Fountain in Glasgow's Kelvingrove Park, constructed to celebrate

the arrival of Glasgow's water supply from Loch Katrine, features statues of nine birds of prey including two owls. There is no direct Verne connection other than that at that time, The Trossachs were renowned for the proliferation of raptors and so Verne was on sound ornithological ground.

13 Marel, H, *Jules Verne, Zola et la mine, in Germinal. Une Documentation Intégrale*, University of Glasgow French and German Publications, 1989.

CHAPTER SEVEN

The Green Ray

VERNE'S LAST NOVEL SET entirely in Scotland, *Le Rayon vert (The Green Ray)*, was published in 1882 in the magazine *Le Temps* before being published by Hetzel in his *Voyages Extraordinaires* collection in the same year. It evoked varying responses from critics, ranging from being considered lightweight and rather silly to charming romance. It seems that Verne's publisher, Hetzel, belonged in the latter camp. Whatever view one takes, certain qualities are generally agreed upon. Of the few novels featuring a romantic heroine, Helena Campbell is one of the most finely drawn. She is portrayed as being a charming if headstrong girl who, when frustrated, can show anger. She has left girlhood behind and in the course of the novel emerges as a woman. She is firm in her view that the choice of a husband concerns herself and no one else. Verne describes her thus:

> In truth, she was charming, her pretty face with blue eyes – the blue of the Scottish lochs.

She was devoted to her home area, to her clan and her family, a common theme in Verne's portrayal of the Scots. Even critics of the literary merit concede that in this novel Verne is at his best in terms of describing landscape, not just as scenery and a backcloth to the action, but evocative of mood, history and culture. Finally, it is now clear that it is in this story that Verne most closely exploits his own experience directly, namely his journey to the Hebrides in 1879. Compared with the inclement weather in 1859, Verne's 1879 journey was blessed with calm and sunny days. This led Verne to make extravagant comparisons between the Hebrides and the Greek islands. While admitting that the Greek archipelago enjoyed deeper shades of blue compared to the misty Scottish islands, nevertheless, the drama of the seascapes and above all the subliminal presence of the Scandinavian gods, Odin, Ossian and Fingal having escaped from the sagas, were a match for the legendary gods of Mount Olympus.

Sam and Sib Melvill, Helena's guardians, are incapable of bridging
the generation gap and understanding her feminine psyche.
L Benett

The brothers Sam and Sib

The story begins in a mansion near Helensburgh owned by two brothers Samuel and Sebastian Melvill. Verne had never set foot in Helensburgh, but had sailed close by in the *Columba* and would have appreciated the magnificent bourgeois villas and mansions on the seafront to the west of the town centre. The brothers have built their 'cottage', as Verne inappropriately terms it, overlooking the Gareloch and across the Clyde to Greenock. They also own a smart town house in the fashionable area of West George Street in Glasgow near to Blythswood Square where they spend the winter months. The two men, Samuel and Sebastian, referred to in the novel by their diminutives of 'Sam' and 'Sib', are the uncles and guardians of Helena Campbell, the orphaned daughter of their sister and the heroine of the story. Verne defines Sam, the elder of the two, as being 'her father' and Sib 'her mother', an allusion which has led some critics to propose a homosexual relationship. This hypothesis is heightened by the fact that Verne enjoyed playing word games; the diminutive 'Sib' when reversed as 'bis' refers in French to 'two', suggesting that the brothers are virtual clones. Whether or not this was Verne's intention is unproven, but what is beyond doubt is their total devotion to the well-being of Helena and above all their ardent desire that, having reached the age of 18, she should find a suitable husband as soon as possible. Already they begin to fantasise about a fashionable wedding at St George's Kirk, close to their Glasgow town house and even have a suitor in mind[1]. He is Aristobulus Ursiclos, a graduate in chemistry and physics of the universities of Oxford and Edinburgh, who turns out to be a pedantic young man whose accident-prone behaviour turns him into a figure of farce. Having decided that Aristobulus would be a suitable future husband, on Helena's return from a walk the brothers propose his name to her. Helena breaks into fits of laughter and states firmly that she will never choose a husband until she has seen the green ray. [FIG. 9]

A newspaper item

The cause of Helena's outburst and the crucial stage of the novel which underpins the rest of the book is an article which Helena has read that morning in the Morning Post. The article gives a description of the

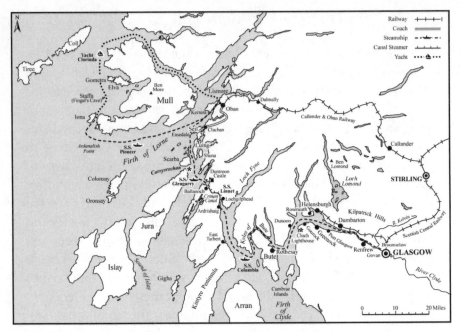

FIG. 9 The itinerary of *The Green Ray*

meteorological phenomenon, the green ray, which in certain atmospheric conditions can appear as the sun dips below the horizon of the sea producing not the rose colour one associates with sunset, but a flash of green light. Moreover, Helena recalls an ancient Highland legend according to which, whosoever witnesses this phenomenon can be sure of their decision in emotional matters and in particular the choice of a marriage partner. As a mariner Verne would probably have been aware of the green ray and the fact that its observation required a clear view of the sea's horizon. Confined by the Rosneath peninsula and by the hills of Arran and Kintyre, there is no chance that Helena can witness the ray from Helensburgh. Accordingly, the uncles propose a journey to Oban, knowing well but not telling Helena, that Aristobulus Ursiclus is presently on holiday there. She agrees immediately and demands that the journey should commence the following day for it is the beginning of August and autumnal mists clouding the horizon will not be long delayed. Sam and Sib give orders to their housekeeper Beth, and man-servant, Partridge, to prepare for the journey, whose duration can only be guessed at.

Helena Campbell, a beautiful but wilful young woman whose
strong personality drives the plot of the novel.

L Benett

Setting sail for Oban

At the crack of dawn, the party climbs aboard the Glasgow train at Helensburgh and an hour later is making its way to the Broomielaw quay where the RMS *Columba* lies waiting for its 8am departure[2]. Verne gives a detailed description of features of the Clyde as the steamer passes Partick, the Kilpatrick Hills, Dumbarton and Cardross on the right bank and Renfrew, Port Glasgow and Greenock on the left before heading south west at Cloch lighthouse into the Firth of Clyde and the open sea[3]. While her uncles admire the changing panorama, Helena becomes more and more frustrated at the lack of a sea horizon and at the realisation that only seven more hours of daylight remain. The *Columba* weaves her way through the Kyles of Bute and turns north into Loch Fyne. Here she makes the last of the many stops on her journey at Tarbert before reaching her journey's end at Ardrishaig. Helena, her uncles and the two servants disembark and walk across the road to join the charming little canal boat, the *Linnet*, on the Crinan Canal. Several hours later, another boat transfer takes place as the passengers on the *Linnet* board the waiting *Glengarry* for the last leg of the journey to Oban[4].

Drama in the Corryvreckan maelström

On rounding the northern point of Jura, Helena gains her first view of an open sea horizon. It is by now six o'clock and time is running out to reach Oban before sunset. Her eyes fixed on the western horizon, she becomes aware of a roaring sound coming from a mighty disturbance in the sea. She asks the captain what this commotion of sound and waves is and he tells her that it is the notorious Corryvreckan whirlpool between Jura and Scarba[5]. Helena's young eyes detect something abnormal within the whirlpool and she assumes that she is looking at a rock. Through his spyglass the captain contradicts her, for it is a small boat trapped in the Corryvreckan and he announces that there are two figures, one apparently unconscious and the other rowing furiously but to little effect. Immediately Helena insists that the *Glengarry* should go to their assistance but the captain explains that his vessel cannot enter the centre of the whirlpool without putting the ship and her passengers in danger. Helena pleads that something must be done to rescue the two unfortunates and she is volubly supported by other passengers watching the unfolding drama. The captain guides the *Glengarry* towards the edge of the Corryvreckan and after a titanic struggle the young oarsman approaches the steamer and clasps a rope. Safely aboard the *Glengarry*, the rescued pair is seen to be an older man, owner of the boat, and a young man whose strength had enabled him to avoid the clutches of the whirlpool. Soon recovered from his ordeal, the young man profusely thanks the captain. Without the *Glengarry* coming to his aid, the boat would inevitably have been dragged to the centre of the whirlpool and capsized as his own strength weakened[6]. The captain brushes aside their thanks and claims that their rescue is owed more to the passengers than to himself. Modestly, Helena draws to the side of the crowd surrounding the young man, not wishing her crucial role in spotting the boat and gathering the support of the passengers to pressure the captain into action to be known.

After this adventure, normality returns as the *Glengarry*, with its additional passengers, steams on to Oban. Sadly for Helena, the commotion of the rescue distracted her from witnessing the green ray and now it is dark. She displays only a little regret and one senses that meeting the young man was more than adequate compensation for this loss and that we are certain to hear and see more of him before long. After this long day which had started so early, the party is delighted to settle in to the best rooms of the Caledonian Hotel on Oban's seafront, and where Verne himself had stayed a mere three years before the publication of the novel.

Frustrations in and around Oban

The following morning, Sam and Sib rise early and take a stroll along the seafront. At this time, Oban was a small town, a former fishing village which, given its strategic location between the Highlands and Hebrides, had developed as a ferry port and embryonic tourist centre. There is every chance that the pair will meet Aristobulus Ursiclos, for this is their intention. Indeed as they expected, they meet him in mid-perambulation on the shore pondering various scientific matters. Verne introduces us to one of the most ridiculous characters he has created. Whereas Paganel in *The Children of Captain Grant* absent-minded and a little eccentric, Ursiclos is practically a schizophrenic, incapable of conducting a normal conversation without introducing esoteric scientific information often of

The captain and passengers of the *Glengarry* view the struggle
for survival of the young man in the Corryvrechan whirlpool.
L Benett

no direct relevance to the subject being discussed. While Paganel evolves
in the course of the novel from being an armchair and dry academic to
being a practical and inventive person, Ursiclos becomes simply more
and more absurd as the plot develops. In the eyes of the uncles however
he has one merit. He comes from a solid bourgeois family and, therefore,

Helena and her uncles establish their headquarters on a seafront hotel
in Oban during their quest for the green ray.

L Benett

is a suitable match for Helena. He is apparently pleased to know that
Helena is with her uncles in Oban, but admits that the green ray is
unknown to him. He does, however, accurately forecast a deterioration
in the weather.

At this point Helena joins the group and is less than thrilled to see Ursiclos, but more importantly she is furious with her uncles. On leaving the hotel she has discovered that no open sea horizon is visible from Oban, the bay being enclosed by the island of Kerrera and the mountainous island of Mull. The party are about to abandon the project but the hotel proprietor Mr MacFyne, anxious to retain the financial patronage of his distinguished guests, suggests that a view of the open sea can be obtained from the island of Seil, a mere four or five miles to the south by the simple expedient of horse and carriage. They agree to stay in Oban, but the bad weather predicted by Ursiclos closes in and makes any excursion to Seil pointless given the overcast sky. Helena spends the next four days strolling on the beach, from time to time sitting on a rock and letting her thoughts stray to the rescue of the young man from the Corryvreckan and recalling that he was indeed a handsome person.

The following day, to her great relief, Helena wakes to magnificent sunshine. With high anticipation, the group sets off at five in the evening in the hotel's horse and carriage southwards to the Isle of Seil[7]. Climbing a hillside, they have an uninterrupted view of the horizon. The sun is slowly sinking when at the crucial moment, a wisp of cloud obscures it and the chance of witnessing the green ray is lost.

The following day, the cloud cover indicates that a return to Seil would be unrewarding. Instead, accompanied by the housemaid Beth, Helena sets out sightseeing. In response to Beth's prompting, Helena expresses her disdain for Ursiclos and discretely asks if anything more has been heard of the young man from the *Glengarry*. The two uncles are by now getting almost as frustrated in their plan to advance the cause of Ursiclos as Helena is in her forlorn search for the green ray. The next morning they organise a game of croquet in which Ursiclos is to partner Helena. The Melvill brothers are outstanding players and soon establish a healthy lead. Helena too plays well, but Ursiclos, relying on a scientific analysis of each shot, is worse than useless, even managing to smite his own ankle with a mighty blow of his mallet! Exasperated by his performance and having lost to her uncles, Helena aims a careless shot with all her force. The ball leaves the croquet lawn and ends up on the beach, striking the palette and upsetting the easel of a young artist. It is none other than the young man rescued from the Corryvreckan!

Helena's reckless angry shot demolishes the easel of
the young man rescued from the Corryvrechan.
L Benett

Oliver Sinclair joins the hunt for the green ray

Verne identifies the artist as Oliver Sinclair, a fine looking 26-year-old man from a prominent Edinburgh family, who, having benefited from an inheritance, had travelled the world before taking up his passion for painting and especially seascapes. Helena and her uncles offer their profuse apologies while Ursiclos, baffled at his inability to transform scientific theory into practice at croquet, leaves the group and sets off for the island of Luing to turn his attention to geological exploration.

A conversation develops with Oliver Sinclair and he learns that his new companions were aboard the *Glengarry* at the time of his rescue and that their sojourn at Oban is in search of the green ray. Sinclair immediately becomes animated, for although he has never heard of the green ray, his passion for painting seascapes leads him to seek the elusive colours of the sea, which is what in fact had tempted him too close to the Corryvreckan in spite of the remonstrations of the Jura fisherman whom he had hired to row him. He announces his intention to join the search and frequently meets Helena over the next few days. At last the barometer rises and Oliver, Helena and her uncles set off once again for the Isle of Seil, full of anticipation. As the sun gradually sinks below the horizon the group hold their breath for the spectacle when they notice a sailing boat leaving Easedale and heading between them and the sunset. At the crucial moment the boat's sail completely blots out the sunset and yet again the green ray is obscured! The boat lands and a figure makes his way over the rocks to join the group. To her horror, Helena recognises Aristobulus Ursiclos and in a towering rage can barely bring herself to speak to him.

A new plan is hatched

After the double failure at the Isle of Seil, Helena, now joined in her obsession by Oliver, considers their strategy. Oliver proposes that rather than pursing the constrained view from Seil, they should sail to the island of Iona with its unrestricted view westwards over the Atlantic. At this point Verne returns to his own journey as the party, including the servants Bess and Partridge, board the *Pioneer* which sets sail from the North Pier at 8am. The steamer sails along the spectacular south coast of Mull and Helena and Oliver are deep in conversation about the marvels of the sea. Oliver is the mouthpiece of Verne's own conviction when he muses;

> I believe that I was born to be a sailor and if since my childhood this was not to be my career I regret it every day.

Compared with this nostalgic recollection, a voice behind them exclaims;

> The sea, a combination of hydrogen and oxygen, with two and a half percent of sodium chloride.

It is none other than Aristobulus Ursiclos! His pedantic analysis of the chemical composition of seawater contrasts with the romantic and passionate evocation of the sea expressed by Helena and Oliver.

More frustration on Iona

At midday the *Pioneer* moors off the jetty of Iona and the passengers are ferried to shore by local boatmen, who gain a small financial supplement to their crofting activity. Here no comfortable hotel awaits them and instead the Helensburgh group are obliged to lodge in an inn, the 'Arms of Duncan[8]' while Ursiclos and Oliver find shelter in a fisherman's cottage. What the inn lacks in comfort it makes up for in the quality of its cuisine. Verne describes, with varying accuracy, a gargantuan dinner featuring all the Scottish dishes and drinks that he had experienced on his two journeys. Four days of poor weather pass by but Helena is far from bored. She is delighted to escape the hurly burly of Oban and is entranced by the magic of the island's scenery and the mystical powers of the ruined cathedral, nunnery and graveyards. Verne gives an almost tourist guide account of the historic site which once more contrasts with the bizarre scientific expostulations of Ursiclos as he examines the mineral composition of the gravestones and paces out dimensions of the ruins.

August gives way to September and still the green ray eludes the group, to the chagrin of Helena and Oliver. However, on 5 September, the barometer rises and clear skies announce a perfect day. In the evening the group assembles on the northernmost hillside of the island. Tension rises as the sun begins to sink below the horizon when suddenly two explosions shatter the calm and clouds of terrified seabirds fly up, forming a screen between the observers and the sun. The origin of the explosion soon

With the ruined Iona cathedral in the background, Helena and her
companions admire the royal tombs.
L Benett

becomes evident. Inevitably it is again Aristobulus Ursiclos, a shotgun in
his hands, who has fired on the birds. What little credibility he had has
now disappeared. Uncles Sam and Sib agree that Ursiclos has exhausted
their patience and Helena simply maintains a tight-lipped silence.

Staffa – the Green Ray at last!

By now Helena has decided that only by escaping from the foolish Aristobulus will she ever witness the green ray. She has already recognised the island of Staffa to the north and asks Oliver if it is possible to visit it. Oliver claims that nothing is easier if one charters a yacht for the purpose. Accordingly he goes to the pier and hires the services of Captain Olduck, master of the sailing yacht *Clorinda*, to set sail for Staffa in the morning[9]. At six o'clock the following morning, the group, minus Aristobulus Ursiclos, embark aboard the yacht. A crew of six, a coxswain and the skipper form the complement of the *Clorinda*. The distance to Staffa is a mere eight miles and in spite of a headwind the *Clorinda* soon reaches the island but the weather is becoming ominous. The yacht anchors off Clamshell Bay and the party goes ashore in her lifeboat.

It does not take long to explore this tiny island and from the summit it is clear that the cloud cover will prevent any sighting of the green ray that evening. The night is spent aboard the *Clorinda*, where sadly the barometer continues to descend. The following day a picnic lunch is taken at Clamshell Bay after which Captain Olduck puts the party ashore at Boat Cave. Here they are sheltered from the gaze of the passengers of the *Pioneer,* anchored off Fingal's Cave while its tourists, like Verne in 1879, take the mandatory two hour trip to this most famous feature. Returning to the *Clorinda* they find Captain Olduck deep in thought. The barometer is continuing to fall and it is clear that a violent storm is approaching. He informs the group that the yacht must seek shelter immediately on the east coast of Mull. Helena is horrified at this latest development, but Oliver proposes that while the *Clorinda* must depart from Clamshell Bay, the passengers could shelter in the cave. Helena persuades her uncles that this course of action is best and all the necessities to survive for a few days are transferred from the *Clorinda*, and she sets sail for shelter on Mull, but leaves behind a small rowing boat in case it could be useful to explore the island. In fact there is no immediate need of this boat for a footpath leads from Clamshell Bay along the rocky coast to Fingal's Cave. Oliver Sinclair leads the group along the path and a ledge with a handrail allows them to penetrate into the depth of the cave. Here Verne, drawing on his own emotions, paints a dramatic evocation of the grandeur of the cave, the music caused by the lapping of the waves and the ancient legends associated with Fingal.

The following day, the storm is at its height. Although the party is marooned due to the weather at its base in Clamshell Bay, Helena, revelling in the wild atmosphere, takes little walks from time to time. The following evening she does not return from one of her walks. The group hastens to Fingal's Cave, which is now lashed by gigantic waves, when to their horror they discover Helena's hair band close to the entrance. Oliver Sinclair and the manservant Partridge hasten back to Clamshell Bay and manhandle the boat, left behind for their use by the *Clorinda*, to the cave entrance. Immediately Oliver launches the rowing boat and begins a Herculean effort to row into Fingal's Cave. Once inside he hears a faint reply to his shouts. Helena is there, and still alive. She has sought refuge in a natural cavity, 'Fingal's Chair', but all means of escape are impossible due to the high tide and the surge of the waves. Oliver leaps on to the rock and clasps Helena in his arms. He murmurs to Helena that it was thanks to her that he was saved from the Corryvreckan and now it his turn to save her from Fingal's Cave. Thus reassured and at the end of her strength, Helena faints in his arms[10]. In effect the storm, which had briefly separated the couple, now reunites them. Oliver calculates that the tide will start to ebb at midnight and eventually this is the case. As the sea level falls, and in spite of the surging swell, the pathway cleft into the rock and protected by a hand rail gradually re-emerges and Oliver can begin his dangerous escape carrying the unconscious Helena over his shoulder. He is greeted at the mouth of the cave by Sam and Sib, Partridge and Bess, who have spent the night there hoping and praying that Helena will be rescued. Once returned to the bracing air of Clamshell Bay, Helena regains consciousness. Oliver Sinclair is a hero, acclaimed by the family and servants and the idea of Aristobulus Ursiclos as a possible suitor has been erased from the minds of Sam and Sib. Gradually Oliver recovers his strength and goes for a walk on the summit plateau of the island[11]. Immediately he realises that the weather is rapidly improving and that the horizon has become clear of cloud. He hurries back to the camp and announces that at last the chances of witnessing the green ray are excellent.

At five o'clock the whole party climbs up to the hilltop and prepares for sunset. Yet again a sail boat appears to the north heading towards the island. Is Ursiclos aboard and once again going to ruin the view? No, this time it is the *Clorinda* and she heads south towards Clamshell Bay to

Helena experiences the awesome spectacle of Fingal's Cave with no premonition that it will soon almost cost her young life.

L Benett

collect the group. The sun is sinking and all eyes are fixed on the horizon. But not quite all, for Helena is gazing into the dark eyes of Oliver and in turn he is transfixed by her deep blue eyes. 'The green ray!' exclaim the uncles, Bess and Partridge, but not Oliver and Helena. They no longer

By a prodigious physical effort Oliver rescues Helena at the limit
of her endurance.
L Benett

need a meteorological affirmation of their true love. Thus the climax of
the story is reached and what follows is almost an anticlimax as if, having
reached a peak of action, Verne seems anxious to finish the novel without
further ado. The following day the *Clorinda* returns the party to Oban

At last the green ray is sighted, but not by Helena and Oliver!
L Benett

where after a last night in the Caledonian Hotel they take the train back to Glasgow and Helensburgh [12]. Eighteen days later Helena and Oliver are married in St George's Church, close to the uncles' town residence. After all the effort and drama, the couple never saw the green ray, but as Helena insists they saw something better – they saw each other!

A *trivial* novel?

To claim that this novel is trivial is too severe a judgement, for each of Verne's Scottish novels has its own particular flavour, characterisation and plot. Moreover Verne's publisher, Hetzel, often critical of his manuscripts, found *The Green Ray* charming. Perhaps Helena Campbell is stereotypical and closely modelled on Lady Helena Glenarvan, but her character has more edge, less patience, and until she meets Oliver Sinclair, she is more self-absorbed. One distinguished critic has gone so far as to regard *The Green Ray* as a feminist novel. Of the various female characters portrayed by Verne, Helena comes closest to being the heroine and principal character of a novel, rather than playing a supporting role to more dominant males.

In discussing the character of Helena with Hetzel, Verne stated that:

> The heroine should be young, but very original, eccentric while still remaining proper and this must be written with a very light touch.

However, the uncles Sam and Sib, clones of each other, and the ridiculous buffoon Aristobulus Ursiclos, are unlike any other of Verne's Scottish characters. One guesses that Verne was writing tongue-in-cheek and attempting to inject an element of farce into the story. The choice of Ursiclos as a suitor for Helena indicates the complete naivety of Sam and Sib and a total lack of judgement, as might be expected of confirmed middle-aged bachelors with little understanding of the fairer sex. Criticism has been made that the novel is too linear, lacking flashbacks or diversions. In fact, given that it follows an established itinerary by boat and train that had been followed by Verne, a degree of linearity is inevitable. As far as the plot is concerned, it may lack depth but it certainly does not lack movement. In addition to the rescue of Oliver, which is a crucial turning point in the story and re-focuses the plot, and the rescue of Helena from Fingal's Cave, which gives the novel its climax, the plot moves along at a gentle pace with occasional twists. This gives Verne the space to add detailed descriptions of scenery and discourses on Scottish history and culture. Finally, even the sternest critic has conceded the quality of Verne's evocation of landscape, weather, mood and atmosphere, especially of the Hebrides. It is clear from correspondence and from interviews, that this part of his 1879 visit remained with him as one of the most memorable journeys in his life. We can thus see *The Green Ray* as being a novel written with affection and recollection which, if not his greatest novel, was nevertheless close to his heart. Moreover, this novel contradicts the view that Verne wrote only for boys. The central theme of the romantic love of a young couple would have appealed equally to girls.

Notes

1 St George's Kirk remains one of the finest buildings of the city centre and a prominent landmark in the skyline. It is located on the former St George's Square, now renamed 'Nelson Mandela Square'. Helena would have reached it by coach on her wedding day in no more than five minutes from her uncles' mansion on Blythswood Square.

2 Verne identifies the ship as being the *Columbia*, probably a typographical error as Verne would have been aware of the connection of Iona with Saint Columba, after whom the steamer was named. The map published in Hetzel's edition of *Le Rayon vert* includes several errors. It omits the passage of the *Columba* through the Kyles of Bute and indicates that the *Glengarry* passed between the Isle of Seil and the mainland. This would have been physically impossible given that a low bridge, 'the bridge over the Atlantic', has existed since 1793 and the depth of water would in any case have been far too shallow for navigation. Ben Nevis is labelled Ben Levis!

3 This is the third time, after *The Blockade Runners* and *The Children of Captain Grant*, that Verne has described the Lower Clyde and in practically identical terms, making use no doubt of the same notes. This description of the Firth of Clyde is, however, more detailed than elsewhere and clearly reflects his first-hand observation from aboard the *Columba* as well as reference to a guidebook. It is however not without inaccuracies. He describes Dumbarton Rock as towering over 500 feet above the Clyde, whereas in fact its height is only 240 feet. Later he gives the height of Goatfell on the Isle of Arran as being almost 800 metres whereas in fact it 874 metres.

4 It is surprising that Verne should have used the *Glengarry* as opposed to the much larger *Chevalier*, which he sailed on himself in 1879. The *Glengarry*, because of its small size and draught, was primarily deployed on the

Caledonian Canal. McCrorie, I, *Steamers of the Highlands and Islands*, Greenock, 1987.

5   The Corryvreckan whirlpool, between Jura and Scarba, results from a tidal anomaly combined with an irregular submarine topography. It is strongest on the flood tide and when combined with westerly winds can produce 15-foot standing waves, extremely hazardous to small vessels.

6   Having already featured the Norwegian maelström in the supposed demise of the *Nautilus* in *Twenty Thousand Leagues under the Sea*, it seems that Verne could not resist exploiting a whirlpool again in *The Green Ray*.

7   Verne gives the time for sunset on 7 August as being 7.54pm. This seems too early for the latitude of Oban. The US Naval Observatory records for this day in 1880 show sunset at 8.25pm. The only way Verne could have arrived at his time would have been using the latitude of Oban but the longitude of Greenwich.

8   No hotel with the name 'Arms of Duncan' is recorded on Iona but at the time of the party's visit, two hotels existed, the 'Columba', built in 1846 and the 'Argyll', built *c.*1870.

9   The choice of the name *Clorinda* has two possible origins. Even though, unusually for Verne, there is no Scottish connection, the name is probably derived from the battle between a crusader knight Tancred and the pagan girl Clorinda. Less likely, the name may have been a corruption of 'Clarinda', the *nom de plume* of Mrs Agnes McLehose in the prolific correspondence with Robbie Burns, ardent but seemingly platonic admirers, which Verne may have been aware of.

10   Verne again uses the device of a young female swooning with emotion as in the case of Nell in *The Underground City*. Verne admitted to his publisher that he had no talent for describing romantic love scenes and regarded them as an interruption to the rapid movement of his plots.

11   The view from the summit of the island would have been familiar to Verne from his 1879 visit. Time was allowed for this in his excursion aboard the *Pioneer*.

12   By this time the Callander and Oban Railway had reached its terminus at Oban, whereas Verne had to take the Royal Mail stagecoach to Dalmally in 1879.

CHAPTER EIGHT

The Fabulous Adventures of Master Antifer

WITH THE PUBLICATION OF *The Green Ray*, Verne accomplished his last novel set entirely in Scotland. One more book, partially set in Scotland, *Mirifiques aventures de Maître Antifer* (*The Fabulous Adventures of Master Antifer*) was published in 1894 but attained a printing of only 7,000 copies. By now, although Verne was 66 years old, his imagination was as lively as ever and over 20 more novels were still to flow from his pen. *The Fabulous Adventures of Master Antifer* returns to several of his favourite themes; long distance voyages, desert islands, colourful characters, a hidden treasure, enigmatic clues and calculations and a solution that depends on geodetic measurements. Only one episode takes place in Scotland, encompassing three chapters, but it is unique in featuring again Verne's beloved Edinburgh, along with the most violent and treacherous action in the story. It is a complex plot with many twists and turns, has a large number of characters and has rather more humour than is normally present in Verne's later books. Even the title word *Mirifiques* (fabulous) adventures suggests that they are barely credible and written tongue-in-cheek, to amuse rather than to instruct.

A fabulous treasure

The plot hangs on the search for a fabulous treasure belonging to a rich Egyptian, Kamylk-Pacha, who, fearing arrest by the Viceroy, Muhammed Ali, hides his fortune on an island and gives clues to its location to four persons who he has decided will be his inheritors. The clues consist of latitudes or longitudes given to individuals to whom he owes a debt of gratitude, but only by combining these clues can the treasure be found. Amongst the recipients of these clues is a retired merchant mariner, a Breton, Pierre-Servan-Malo Antifer, known to his friends and relatives as Maître Antifer[1]. His father had saved Kamylk-Pacha from death and on his own demise had passed on to his son a scrap of parchment containing the figures of a line of latitude. He realises that it is a clue to wealth, but without the corresponding longitude he is powerless to identify where he should search. In effect Verne is recycling the same enigma of a missing line of latitude or longitude as he had used in *The Children of Captain Grant*.

Out of the blue, Antifer receives a visit from an Egyptian lawyer, Ben-Omar, who attempts to purchase the details of the line of latitude from him. Ben-Omar has the corresponding longitude and rather than sell his own information, Maître Antifer agrees to share the information which reveals the location of an island in the Gulf of Oman. At this point the number of adventurers increases as Antifer is accompanied on the search by his nephew, Juhel, and by his old friend Trégomain. Ben-Omar is accompanied by an assistant, Nazim, who in fact is Saouk, the son of Kamylk's treacherous cousin and who is determined to lay his hands on the treasure himself. The details of longitude and latitude lead the treasure hunters to an island off Muscat. Here, rather than treasure, they find the detail of another longitude and the name of Zambuco, a Tunisian banker of Maltese origin, another heir, who holds the corresponding latitude. Zambuco agrees to reveal his secret provided that Antifer, a confirmed bachelor, agrees to marry his Maltese sister![2] Given the choice between losing the fortune or marrying an unprepossessing wife of a certain age, Antifer agrees to the marriage and on exchanging clues the treasure hunt continues. Another island is involved, this time in the Bay of Ma-Yumba, in the Gulf of Guinea off the west coast of Africa. Again the search is inconclusive, yielding only yet another longitude and the name 'Tyrcomel' in Edinburgh. At last, Verne is on familiar ground and the whole cast assemble in his favourite Scottish city: Antifer, Trégomain, Juhel, Zambucco, Ben-Omar and Saouk. Antifer and his friends take rooms in Gibbs Royal Hotel[3] and to their astonishment discover that the possessor of the next clue is none other than a reputed clergyman, the Reverend Tyrcomel, minister of the Tron Church and residing at 17 North Bridge Street, adjacent to the house of John Knox[4].

The sinfulness of wealth!

The easiest way to contact Tyrcomel and to persuade him that they could offer him a chance to gain riches is to attend his church. Accordingly, Antifer, Trégomain, Zambuco, Ben-Omar, Saouk and Juhel listen to his sermon in a packed church. Of the group, only Juhel has a command of English and he cannot believe his ears as the minister launches into a vitriolic tirade against the evil of wealth, inviting kings to give up their civil list, queens to burn their jewellery and the rich to destroy their wealth. Clearly to appeal to Tyrcomel to yield his clue in return for a share in the treasure is unlikely to gain his favour.

At the close of the sermon the group attempts to intercept the minister, but leaving by a side door he has disappeared. To pursue their chase the group decides to visit the minister's house at 17 North Bridge Street.

The following day, Antifer, Zambuco and Juhel set off to seek a meeting with the minister. Tyrcomel's house does not face on to the Canongate but is on the third floor of an eight storey tenement block overlooking the railway. The approach to the house is via a dismal close and the general appearance is one of poverty and misery such as Verne had witnessed on his 1859 visit. The trio climbs a wooden staircase with a rope balustrade and knocks on the minister's door. After a long pause, he opens a slat in the door and demands what they want. When Antifer replies that it is a business matter Tyrcomel declares that he has no interest in business. When Maître Antifer affirms that they have listened to his sermon, the minister, thinking that they are possible converts to his thinking, opens the door and admits them to his stark room, devoid of the slightest comfort. Eventually Juhel, with his command of English, comes to the point and questions the minister if his father had ever known Kamylk-Pacha. Tyrcomel replies in the affirmative and admits that his father had received a clue from the Pacha which would lead to his buried treasure. A heated discussion ensues in which the minister stubbornly refuses to entertain any possibility of revealing his clue to them. As far as he is concerned the corrupting power of wealth is an article of faith. To reinforce his point of view he declares that he has burnt the letter containing the latitude and without further ado obliges the men to leave.

The reverend Tyrcomel refuses to divulge the next clue to the treasure hunt
much to the fury of the searchers.

G Roux

A *violent incident*

Utterly exhausted physically and morally, Maître Antifer has to take to his bed with fever and hallucinations. It seems that the obduracy of the minister will cause them to abandon the hunt. At this point Verne cannot resist repeating his own appreciation of Edinburgh through the eyes of Antifer's friend Trégomain. Obliged to stay in the hotel to look after Antifer he dreams of his desire to follow the Canongate to the Palace of Holyrood, to climb Arthur's Seat and admire the view from the summit. Confined to the hotel room, he is reduced to staring at the Scott Monument and along Princes Street to Calton Hill. Meanwhile, rumours abound that the Reverend Tyrcomel has turned down the opportunity to gain a fortune. Admiration for this man of principle rises to new heights and at his next sermon at the Tron Church the congregation spills over into the adjoining streets. His appearance is greeted by tumultuous applause, but among the congregation one man, concealed behind a pillar, does not join in this adulation. It is a man of about 35-years-old, with black hair and beard and a hard expression on his face. When Tyrcomel makes his way back to his room, the stranger follows him, silently climbing the stairs behind the minister and concealing himself in a dark corner.

The following morning the minister's neighbours are surprised that Tyrcomel does not appear outside at his habitual early hour. By the afternoon he has still not appeared and the police are called, who force the door only to be confronted with a horrific sight. The room has been ransacked, the table overturned, drawers pulled out and their contents scattered on the floor. An unconscious Tyrcomel, his hands savagely tied behind his bare back, is sprawled across the bed. The constables rush to revive him and on massaging his back reveal an inscription on his left shoulder. It is a tattoo of a value of latitude, 77 degrees 19 minutes North! It had been inscribed by his father while Tyrcomel was still a child and he had never paid any attention to it. As he regains his senses, the minister is able to tell the police that his assailant was none other than one of the strangers who had attempted to persuade him to reveal his clue to the location of Kamylk-Pacha's treasure. The police hasten to commence their inquiry and the group are traced to Gibb's Royal Hotel. Fortunately Antifer, Juhel, Tregomain, Zambucco and Ben-Omar have faultless alibis for none of them had left the hotel. It is evident that the culprit was Saouk

The horrific sight which greets the rescuers of the reverend Tyrcomel with the map references tattooed on his back.

G Roux

and that he is now in possession of the latitude to add to the longitude discovered at Ma-Yumba. Clearly his plan is to hurry to the treasure site and claim it for himself. However all is not lost, for the following day the local press report the drama, including the reading of the latitude found on Tyrcomel's back. Quickly the treasure searchers consult their atlas and discover that the longitudes found at Ma-Yumba coupled with this latitude locate a further island, Spitsbergen.

The end of the search

At this point the Scottish section of the novel is over. Antifer loses no time in discovering that there are steamer links between Leith and Bergen and from there to Hammerfest. To travel onwards to Spitsbergen it would be necessary to charter a boat at some expense. Zambucco, the Tunisian banker, is able to draw a considerable sum from the Bank of Scotland and with their finances replenished, the following day the group catches a tram to Leith and boards the tramp steamer *Viken* bound for Bergen. The remainder of the plot does not concern our interest in Scotland and can be summarised briefly. After a frustrating voyage, for the steamer makes many points of call along the Norwegian fiords, the *Viken* arrives at Hammerfest, safely avoiding the Maelström. Here the group books into the North Pole Hotel and searches for a boat owner willing to take them the 600 miles to Spitsbergen. They manage to hire a fishing vessel, the *Kroon*, a 100 ton vessel with a crew of 11. The clues to the treasure indicate a location on the most southerly island of the archipelago. The group are put ashore and immediately find the treasure site, marked as usual by Kamylk-Pacha's signature on a rock. To the dismay of the hunters, the box that they unearth contains no treasure but another message indicating that the treasure is located on yet another island and to the fury of Antifer, the part of the message that indicates the last hiding place is too damaged to be legible.

In disgust the Frenchmen make their way back to Brittany, while Zambuco returns to Tunis and Ben-Omar to Alexandria. The treasure remains undiscovered, but at least Antifer escaped the arranged marriage with Zambuco's sister. On the other hand, Juhel is free to marry Antifer's niece, Enogate. Here, Verne gives a penultimate twist to the story. As Juhel points out on a globe to his new wife the route that the treasure seekers have followed, Enogate traces it with her finger. She suddenly exclaims that she knows where the fourth island, the hiding place of the treasure, is located! The enigma is solved because the longitudes and latitudes which defined the three islands describe the circumference of a circle and by extending lines at right angles from each point it is possible to identify at their intersection an island in the western Mediterranean between Sicily and Pantelleria. Maître Antifer is informed of Enogate's discovery and telegrams are sent to Zambuco and Ben-Omar giving a rendezvous in Sicily as close as possible to the treasure island. Assembled once more, the group hires a felucca, the *Providenza*, and set sail for the final coordinates of latitude and longitude. Verne now gives the plot a final twist. To their consternation no island is to be found and Antifer interrogates the captain. In broken French he explains that there was an island, the île Julia, produced by a submarine eruption, but that 31 years ago this island had sunk below the surface of the sea[5]. Antifer's patience is now totally exhausted and he gives the command to return to Sicily, knowing now that the treasure is lost forever.

Another version of the Scottish character?

It is difficult to characterise this novel. It is fast-moving, there are elements of farce, there is tension and distrust between the French and the other treasure seekers and a dénouement which, while disappointing as it ends in failure, also contains a moral. In effect one suspects that Verne's personal views, though much less extreme, are more closely aligned with those of the Reverend Tyrcomel than with the avarice of the searchers. Tyrcomel is unique in Verne's portrayal of Scottish characters. He is austere, cold, implacable in his hatred of wealth and despite his immense popularity with his congregation, he is a gloomy, forbidding character who appears to hold the view that pleasure has no place in this existence. This is totally at odds with, for example, Lord Glenarvan, who exploits his wealth in the service of others. The choice of Edinburgh as the setting for the Scottish episode corresponds with Verne's knowledge of macabre events in the city's past and his awareness of its importance in ecclesiastical history. In fact, his treatment of Edinburgh carries more conviction than the episodes in the exotic islands. Certainly in terms of character portrayal, he puts more effort into the depiction of Tyrcomel than any of the other personalities with the partial exception of Maître Antifer himself. It is sad nevertheless that Verne's final Scottish character should have been such an unappealing person. His other melancholic character, Silfax, at least had the virtue of dedication to the care of orphan Nell and a lifetime of commitment to the mine as redeeming features.

Notes

1   Verne had passed an enjoyable holiday near Dinard in 1893 and the names of some of the characters in the novel reflect place names in this part of Brittany. St Malo and St Servan are located across the Rance estuary from Dinard and St Enogat is a beach settlement within walking distance of Verne's holiday home. Enogat is feminised in the novel to Enogate, the name of Antifer's niece. Antifer is a headland on the coast to the north of Le Havre and well known to Verne, while Trégomain is a village to the west of Nantes which would also have been known to Verne. Verne used the month-long holiday to complete the first volume of the *Mirifiques aventures de Maître Antifer.*

2   This, and a further reference to Malta in the text, reflect Verne's visit to Malta in 1884 and near shipwreck there.

3   Gibb's Royal Hotel existed in reality on Prince's Street opposite the Scott Monument.

4   Verne had seen the imposing 17th century Tron Kirk in 1859, having twice taken lunch nearby, so it was natural to select it as a location. However, after the 'disruption' of 1843 when the Free Church split from the Church of Scotland, the Tron Kirk retained its allegiance to the original Church and therefore Verne was erroneous in placing the 'Free' Church minister Tyrcomel in charge of The Tron. In 1862, the date of the action in Edinburgh, the minister of the Tron Kirk was the Reverend Andrew Milroy and so the

name Tyrcomel was entirely fictitious. The novel is set in 1862 at which time there existed the 'Auld' (old) Tron Kirk belonging to the Church of Scotland, and a much more modest 'New' Tron Kirk belonging to the Free Church of Scotland, which Verne was not aware of. To suit the plot, Verne used the Church of Scotland Tron Kirk but transposed a fundamentalist minister from the nearby but inconspicuous 'Free' Tron Kirk. William Findlay, *The Tron Kirk, Edinburgh*, Edinburgh, 1879.

5 Verne had already made reference to this disappeared island in *Le Chancellor*, 1875, (*The Survivors of the Chancellor*).

CHAPTER NINE

Then and Now: In the Scottish Footsteps of Jules Verne

IT IS NOW 131 YEARS since the *St-Michel III* left her mooring in the port of Leith and set sail for France. Jules Verne departed Scotland for the last time on the morning of 23 July 1879. Published references in English to his visits to Scotland are few and far between and often inaccurate. Similarly, awareness of his Scottish novels is relatively sparse in Scotland. Unsurprisingly there is no Scottish 'Verne Trail' or other manifestation of his travels, nor indeed any appreciation of what his Scottish roots meant to him. This chapter attempts to define what is left of the Scotland that Verne experienced. If his spirit were to return, what would Verne still recognize, and in turn what experiences can today's observer share with him?

Edinburgh, Verne's Mecca

The term 'Mecca' is not too strong to apply to the fascination which the city exerted over Verne's psyche. The introduction was not auspicious. He woke from a deep, exhausted slumber as the train from Liverpool pulled into Lothian Street Station and he emerged into a dark Edinburgh and pouring rain. The loss of the original Lothian Street Station was not a disaster since it was no more than a four platform wooden shanty. But from the moment he woke the following morning and gazed from the hotel window at the panorama of the Old Town against the backcloth of Arthur's Seat, his romance with Edinburgh was born. It was his first encounter with a Scottish city, and it was here that he made his first Scottish friends and his first tangible encounter with his hero, Sir Walter Scott, whose memorial he saw from his bedroom window.

It would still be easy for Verne to replicate his first walk with his friend Hignard and to recognise the landmarks en route. Changes in the streetscape abound, it is true. Lothian Road Station no longer exists and the Grassmarket is now lined with cafes and restaurants leading to the tourist epicentre of the Royal Mile. The Tron Kirk, which he imagined resounded to the exhortations of the Reverend Tyrcomel, recently became a tourist information office before being closed altogether at the time of writing. St Giles' Cathedral, unloved by Verne because of its austerity, still dominates the High Street and the supposed house of John Knox still stands, but it is in the Canongate that he would observe the most fundamental change. Gone are the noisome poverty stricken streets and closes. Improved public hygiene and subsequent gentrification ensure that the contrast between the Canongate and the High Street is no longer so stark. The new and ultra modern Scottish Parliament building would astonish him, although he would be delighted by the political devolution of Scotland leading to its construction. Leaving aside the traffic and tourist flows, the New Town would not be architecturally foreign to Verne's memory. Similarly, Inverleith Row, the magnificent Botanic Gardens and Warriston Cemetery would still be familiar. The viewpoints that Verne scaled, the Castle Esplanade, Calton Hill, and above all Arthur's Seat, are all still accessible although the vistas now include extended suburbs that did not exist in Verne's day. The pall of smoke which constantly hung over 'Auld Reekie' is mercifully no longer in evidence since the end of the use of coal for domestic purposes. It is at the coast of the Firth of Forth that he would be possibly confused. A marina has replaced the ferry and steamer services at Granton and Newhaven is no longer a quaint fishing port, but a conservation area and residential suburb. Leith has experienced considerable regeneration of the dock area, including leisure facilities and eateries, and Portobello has lost much of its function as a fashionable and thriving tourist resort and is also now primarily a residential suburb. Of the various towns and cities that Verne visited, it was Edinburgh that he left with regret in 1859 and it was his first and last port of call in 1879. It is doubtful that he would approve of the extent to which banal forms of tourism have transformed scenes in the Old Town that he associated with stirring historical events and the settings for Sir Walter Scott's heroes, but at least he would find the fundamental structure of the core area of the city clearly recognisable, and to such a keen observer of his surroundings, he would have no difficulty in recreating his epic walk of 27 August 1859.

West Fife

It is a simple matter to reconstruct the route followed by Verne, Hignard and the Reverend Mr Smith from Crombie Point to Oakley on 29 August 1859, although the actual tract of their walk has been fundamentally changed with the disappearance of lanes and altered field boundaries. The jetty at Crombie point is now derelict and no longer served by steamers and the Black Anchor Tavern, where the group sheltered and had a drink, is now a modernised private house. Inzievar House, where Verne and Hignard enjoyed a marathon lunch, is externally much the same as in 1859 but has been converted into flats and access is strictly private. The railway where Verne caught the train to Stirling closed to passengers in 1968, but the track bed is still in use as a cycle route. The ironworks at Oakley, which so impressed Verne, closed a decade after his visit. The memory of his visit lives on however, thanks to community celebrations organised by the Archivists of Dunfermline Council in August 2009, which successfully recreated the visit and received much media coverage.

Glasgow – the point of departure

Verne spent only two nights in total in Glasgow, but as a young man determined not to waste a minute, he covered much of the north bank of the city in 1859, on foot and by coach, and encompassing the medieval core, the city centre, the port and part of the new western bourgeois suburbs. His feelings about Glasgow were ambivalent. He admired the architecture of the city centre buildings, the energy of a city undergoing rapid industrialisation and he saw in the bustling port activity a mirror image of Liverpool. On the other hand, the squalor of the original nucleus of the city, with its open drains and sordid housing, disturbed him and he was disappointed that the cathedral was closed. So much for 'knock and it shall be opened' he mused ironically in 1859. His disappointment was all the greater for he was aware that here was a religious monument dating from the 12th century that had not been disfigured by the Reformation. Today he would find that the slums have disappeared, that the cathedral now extends a day long welcome to visitors and that the arteries of the medieval town are now undergoing regeneration, although undeniably the city's centre of gravity is now firmly anchored in the 19th century 'new town' to the west. One district would be readily recognised by him, although he could not find it on his map in 1859. The Park area dominating Kelvingrove Park had its origins as a bourgeois district high above the Clyde and upwind of the polluted industrial East End. In the latter part of the 20th century, the middle-class families tended to disperse further from the city, as the mansions were too large for smaller families with no further need for domestic servants and coachmen, who had inhabited the mews behind the fine terraces. Residences were replaced by business offices and professional services, but at the present time there is a clear return towards residential accommodation and even the neglected mews are being gentrified into bijou residences. Verne would now find the district quite familiar as compared with 20 or so years ago.

The biggest, and for Verne probably the most disappointing change, would be the Clyde itself. No longer is the Broomielaw the scene of frantic steamer traffic. On both sides of the Clyde the port industrial complexes have disappeared, and in particular the huge conglomeration of port-related activities behind the Anderston and Pointhouse Quays. Tod and McGregor's Meadowside shipyard no longer exists and only in Govan would Verne still be able to see the relic of what Glasgow was like in the 19th century: the building of ships for the entire world. Sadly, shipbuilding now survives only in the form of construction of warships, and is for the British military to a greater extent than for worldwide markets.

If Verne delighted in Edinburgh and had mixed feelings about Glasgow, it is paradoxical that his Scottish novels feature Glasgow to a much greater extent than the national capital. Several reasons may be proposed to explain this contradiction. With its port and estuary, Glasgow was a natural gateway to the great maritime routes of the Atlantic. In this sense it provided an excellent, even dramatic, start for adventure stories involving sea voyages, and equally a haven for a safe return. Glasgow therefore had a certain logic as a point of departure and triumphant return as compared with Edinburgh where port traffic was restricted to the less exciting coastwise and North Sea routes. A particularity of the port of Glasgow was its connection with colonial trade. The city, and especially its merchants and ship owners, grew rich on the American tobacco trade until the War of Independence and on cotton until the American Civil War. This gave Verne the opportunity to invoke global themes, colonisation and slavery for example, and to inveigh against 'English' imperialism, although Scotland was curiously exempt from this criticism.

Within the sector of manufacturing in Glasgow, Verne reserves pride of place for shipbuilding. In *The Blockade Runners* we find specific detail of the history of steam navigation and shipbuilding on the Clyde and he accurately names and locates enterprises such as Napier's engine works and Tod and McGregor's shipyard. Symbolically, the birth of the *Dolphin* launches the novella. Moreover, the location of Glasgow enables Verne to draw on another favourite theme, the landscape and people of the Highlands. The city is a stone's throw from the Highlands and the Clyde is a natural routeway to the mountains and lochs. Perhaps, and most importantly, Verne witnessed in Glasgow echoes of his native Nantes that so fascinated him as a child. The parallels could not be closer: the importance of colonial trade concentrated on the *Quai de la Fosse* in Nantes recalls Steamboat Quay in Glasgow Harbour, the need to improve and dredge the deep water channel applied equally to the Loire and the Clyde, the outport of Paimboeuf being equivalent to Port Glasgow on the Clyde. The industries on the Clyde mirrored those of Nantes including the shipyards of Dubigeon and Babin where his beloved *St-Michel* III was renovated to his orders. In fact it is difficult to see how Verne could have envisioned his Scottish novels without the existence of Glasgow.

Queen Victoria would not be amused! The end of the Royal Route

Apart from his visit to Iona and Staffa, the sea journey from Glasgow to Oban was probably the most memorable of Verne's travels in Scotland. Accomplished entirely on water, he had time to absorb the route as compared with the speed of trains and the rush of horse drawn coaches. Verne would now be able to follow only part of this journey and in fragmented form. Known initially as 'The Royal Route' after Queen Victoria's journey in 1847, and later marketed by MacBrayne as 'The Columba Route', the steamer journey to Oban was first overtaken by rail by the Callander and Oban Railway, The West Highland Railway and then by omnibus and by private car. The nearest equivalent today would be to sail

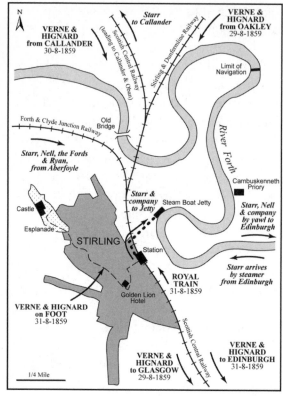

the Clyde on the PS *Waverley*, the paddle steamer launched in 1946 and which spends the summer months sailing a variety of itineraries between the Clyde resorts and sea lochs, including the passage through the Kyles of Bute. Sadly, the Crinan Canal is no longer plied by commercial passenger boats and is limited to pleasure craft. The charming *Linnet* suffered the ignominy of being transformed into a clubhouse for the Glasgow Motor Boat Racing Club in 1930, before sinking in the Gareloch in a storm in 1932.

FIG. 10 Jules Verne's Stirling

Stirling, the crossroads city

Until one draws a map of Jules Verne's references to Stirling, where he spent just one night, it is easy to overlook the extent to which this small city was central to both his own travels and to the itineraries in his writing. On the other hand this simply reflects the fact that by virtue of its geography, Stirling is the national crossroads of Scotland, the crucial link between Highland and Lowland Scotland and centrally located on the most northerly east–west link between the Forth and Clyde valleys. Reflecting this strategic location, Stirling is dominated by a mighty castle and its immediate hinterland includes numerous battlefields, one of which, Bannockburn, is mentioned by Verne in *Backwards to Britain*.

Stirling was at the coalescence of railway routes to all points of the compass and all of which feature in Verne's own and fictional travels. The spine of the system was the Scottish Central line from Perth to Edinburgh and Glasgow, on which various branch lines converged at Stirling. Verne arrived from Oakley via the Dunfermline and Stirling Railway in 1859, and returned from Loch Katrine via the Dunblane, Doune and Callander Railway to Stirling and onwards via the Scottish Central Railway to Edinburgh. Starr, Nell, the Fords and Ryan reached Stirling via the Forth and Clyde Junction railway before embarking on the Forth at the Steamboat Jetty for Edinburgh. This proliferation of private railway companies resulted in Stirling station having three platforms leading to Verne's confusion when changing trains in 1859.

Verne would have little difficulty in orientating himself in present day Stirling. The station occupies the same site but was completely rebuilt in 1912 and was expanded to ten platforms. The Golden Lion still exists, albeit transformed from the hostelry of 1859 into a high quality hotel. The view from the castle esplanade still reveals the mountain setting and the majestic 'links' of the meandering Forth noted by Verne as lengthening the steamer travel time experienced by James Starr aboard the *Prince of Wales*. Steamboat Jetty sadly has disappeared, but the small park that has replaced it enables us to reconstruct Starr's arrival and five minute walk along Shore Road to the railway station.

Oban – Gateway to the Isles

Jules Verne spent two nights in Oban in 1879, but little of that time was spent in exploring the town. His arrival by the PS *Chevalier* from Crinan, threading its way past the islands of Luing, Seil and Kerrera with the Isle of Mull across the Firth of Lorne to the west, gave him a detailed picture of the geography of this complex piece of coastline. But his priority was to take the first opportunity to visit Iona and Staffa. He would see little exactly familiar to him on Iona today. St Columba's Cathedral, which he witnessed as a ruin, is now fully restored and a focus for pilgrims and tourists alike. His fictitious 'Arms of Duncan Hotel' has been replaced in reality by two quality hotels. Staffa, on the other hand is virtually unchanged. Protected originally by private ownership until 1986, when it was gifted to The National Trust for Scotland as a designated National Nature Reserve, Verne would find his enchanted island much the same as when he was mesmerised by Fingal's Cave, although for safety reasons, penetration into the cave where Helena cowered against the far wall may be restricted. However, he would not be able to repeat his leisurely steamer day excursion. No longer could he circumnavigate Mull. Excursions now cross the Sound of Lorne by steamer to Craignure on Mull and passengers are then transported by bus across the island to Fionphort and thence by modern small boats to Iona and Staffa.

His circumnavigation of Mull took a whole day, leaving little time to explore Oban before leaving for Edinburgh by coach and train early the following day. Detailed descriptions of the town are thus lacking in *The Green Ray*. Apart from mention of the Caledonian Hotel, a stone's throw from the North Pier where he boarded the *Pioneer*, and the park where the croquet competition and the reunion with Oliver Sinclair took place, Verne tells us little about the town. In a sense this is unremarkable, for Oban to him was the gateway to the Isles, and the land mattered less than the sea. If Stirling was the crossroads of land routes, so Oban was the equivalent with respect to sea navigation and the door key to the magical Hebrides. A visitor to Oban today would not fail to miss the Caledonian Hotel, the largest and most prestigious hotel on the seafront, and might reasonably assume that this is where Verne and his companions stayed. In fact, this Caledonian Hotel was not completed until 1882, and being adjacent to the newly-arrived railway was predictably named the Station Hotel originally. Verne's Caledonian Hotel, at the junction of the sea front and Argyll Street, no longer exists, largely because it became a victim of its own success. The addition of an extra floor to increase the hotel's capacity to take full advantage of the town's burgeoning tourist traffic put too great a strain on the structure. Built on inadequate foundations on the loose rock of the raised beach, the building was judged unsafe and the property was converted into residential apartments. The name of 'Caledonian' was thus free to be appropriated by the Station Hotel; a more resonant name and entirely appropriate given its location adjacent to the terminus of the Caledonian Railway. The conversion to apartments of Verne's Caledonian Hotel was but a temporary arrangement and eventually demolition was required. This was delayed by the influence of two powerful retail businesses at street level who managed to postpone destruction by removing the upper storeys and sealing the roof but eventually demolition was carried out in the early 1970s. Verne would therefore not

be able now to redis-
cover the hotel that was
the springboard for his
Staffa adventure and he
would surely be horrified
by the utterly undistin-
guished architecture of
the two storey concrete
shop buildings which
have replaced the old
Caledonian Hotel and
which do nothing to
enhance the harmony of
the seafront. As compen-
sation, he would now be

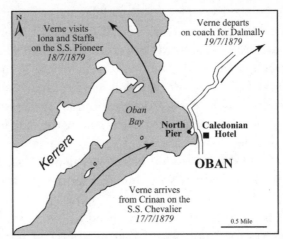

FIG. 11 Jules Verne's Oban

able to take the train from Oban, as compared with the long coach journey to the 1879 railhead at Dalmally.

Loch Lomond and The Trossachs

It is ironic that although Loch Lomond and The Trossachs are among
the best known names on the tourist map of Scotland, and have been
exploited for this purpose since Thomas Cook launched his tourist circuit
in the mid-19th century, Jules Verne would have no difficulty orientating
himself today. In fact both Loch Lomondside and especially Loch Katrine
are remarkably free of the excesses of modern construction related to
tourism. In part this reflects planning controls, and in the case of Loch
Katrine, the function as Glasgow's water supply has rejected any polluting
activity close to the Loch. In fact, the tunnels taking the water from
Loch Katrine to Glasgow were inaugurated by Queen Victoria little more
than a month after Verne's visit in 1859.

The designation of the Loch Lomond and The Trossachs National
Park in 2002 gives hope that the unspoilt character may be preserved.
Certainly some of the features observed by Verne have disappeared. No
longer does a large steamer ply Loch Lomond from Balloch and indeed
the pier railway station has long since closed. A year round steamer
service to the pier at Inversnaid no longer exists and is replaced between

March and December by a small launch from Inveruglas serving the hotel twice per day. Nevertheless, plans are under consideration to reintroduce a steamer service from Balloch to Inversnaid calling at the same piers as Verne experienced. The hotel itself, where Verne enjoyed a whisky and admired the adjacent waterfall in 1859, has been substantially extended. The spectacular view from the hotel of the 'Arrochar Alps' is still much as Verne saw and exulted over, naming the individual peaks in *Backwards to Britain*.

From the Inversnaid Hotel, Verne progressed by horse drawn coach to Stronachlachar. No public transport follows this route any more but the vista along it is still as Verne experienced in pouring rain, which did not dampen his spirits since ahead of him lay Loch Katrine, the spiritual home of Sir Walter Scott by virtue of his epic poem *The Lady of the Lake*. Here again, certain features have changed. The Stronachlachar Hotel was inundated when the water level of Loch Katrine was raised to augment Glasgow's water supply and was never rebuilt. The quaint but very small *Rob Roy* steamer, admired by Queen Victoria, was replaced by the much larger *Sir Walter Scott* in 1900. The Trossachs Hotel, newly opened in 1859, still adds its baronial-style bulk to the landscape albeit transformed into time-share flats. The coach and horses service from Callander to The Trossachs Pier continued until 1937, but is now only accessible by tourist bus or private car. Verne could no longer take the train from Callander to Stirling for this line was closed in 1965 and the handsome alpine chalet style station site has been cleared to make way for a car park. The same sad fate has befallen the Aberfoyle station, where James Starr and his friends set off for Stirling. It closed in 1951 and is now obliterated by car parking.

There is then no 'Verne Trail' for the simple reason that it would now be a fragmented journey and a car would be necessary to link up the various components rather than the integrated travel by train, canal and steamer that was available to Jules Verne. It could be argued that the Verne connection has been neglected by the national and local tourist boards, and that for French visitors in particular, knowledge of Verne's travels and the sites of his novels would add to their Scottish experience.

Epilogue

WITH THE PUBLICATION OF *Mirifiques Aventures de Maître Antifer* in 1894, Verne's 'Scottish' writing had come to a close. Scotland was far from banished from his thoughts, but for a variety of reasons it was never to feature again as a setting for a novel. Several reasons can be suggested to explain why Scotland never again became a muse for his pen. The most likely explanation is simply that he had exploited as settings for his novels all the parts of Scotland that he had seen at first hand. Including *Backwards to Britain*, Glasgow had been featured three times, the Clyde Estuary three times, Edinburgh three times and Loch Lomond and The Trossachs twice. A certain amount of repetition was becoming evident in his texts. Perhaps a more fundamental explanation may have been the deterioration in his state of health and morale. In spite of the impression that might be given by Verne's passion for sailing the high seas and his capacity for sustained hard work on his research and manuscripts, in fact throughout much of his life his health was far from robust. Since adolescence he had been plagued by intestinal troubles and as a young man suffered from facial paralysis. However, his troubles assumed an altogether different dimension in 1886 when on 9 March, Verne was confronted outside his house by his 26-year-old favourite nephew Gaston, who had accompanied him on the 1879 tour of Scotland, who inexplicably shot his uncle in the foot. The incident was reported in Britain in the *Daily Telegraph* on the following day.

> M. Jules Verne, the author of many wondrous tales which have been the delight of old and young, has just had a narrow escape for his life. Yesterday, as he was returning home from a walk, two revolver shots were fired at him, and he was wounded, fortunately not severely, in the left foot. His assailant was his own nephew, M. Gaston Verne, a young man of 25, who is studying in Paris, and who had proceeded to Amiens – where M. Jules Verne is living – without giving any notice of his visit, for the express purpose of attacking his uncle. This sinister design is attributed to a mental obliquity which appears to be making giant strides in this country, and which is euphemistically defined

as 'the monomania of persecution'. As a matter of fact, M. Jules
Verne had always shown the utmost kindness to his relative.

This fit of madness, which has not yet been conclusively explained,
inflicted a serious wound which failed to heal, and the bullet was never
removed, which left Verne lame and in pain for the rest of his life. Nevertheless, the evidence of a mental derangement is clear and Gaston was
to spend the remainder of his life in institutional care. To add to this
grief, a mere eight days later his publisher and close friend Hetzel died.
He was as much a surrogate father as literary mentor to Verne, his own
father having died in 1871. A few months later, in February 1887, Verne
lost his much-beloved mother. He had always been closer to her than to
his father and she was his counsellor and confidante. Her death was a
bitter blow to an already depressed Verne. His supposed mistress, Estelle
Hénin-Duchesne, had already died in 1865. He gained little support in
the face of grief from his son Michel, who had never found stable employ-
ment, was a financial strain on Verne's resources and had eloped with a girl
of 16 in 1883. In 1886 he divorced her for an actress with whom he added
a third child to the two from his previous marriage. Michel, therefore,
was a cause of both material and mental strain on his despairing parent.
To add to these depressing family circumstances, Verne suffered personal
disappointments. It was clear to him that his financial circumstances
were not proportionate to the vast number of his books and their worldwide popularity. In spite of his fame, he did not experience great wealth
and his personal fortune was never more than comfortable. An even
greater cause of chagrin was his feeling that he was insufficiently recognised by his peers as a major literary figure. He aspired to membership
of *l'Académie française*, the pinnacle of literary eminence in France, but
was never elected. The award of *Chevalier dans l'Ordre de la Légion
d'Honneur* in 1870 and promotion to the grade of *Officier* in 1892 were
some consolation, but he would have valued the recognition of his literary
peers more. In addition, the decoration was awarded for his services as
a town councillor at Amiens rather than for his success as an author.

The toll of this period of trauma was the exacerbation of diabetes and
his health progressively deteriorated until his death in 1905. One by one
his relatives and contemporaries passed away, including his devoted
brother Paul in 1897, and a year later his travelling companion and

An undated photograph of Jules Verne wearing the ribbon
of the *Légion d'honneur.*
Courtesy *Société de Géographie de Paris*

artistic collaborator, Aristide Hignard, who had accompanied him to Scotland in 1859. To add to his tribulations, his eyesight deteriorated through a cataract, an immense frustration for a man who had read voraciously all his life, and who had handwritten, through numerous iterations, all his manuscripts. The *St-Michel III*, which in some respects was his escape from his habitual routine and a source of new experiences that he could transform into fiction, had been sold in 1885, when the cost of its physical maintenance and the expense of a very large crew exceeded Verne's capacity to finance his passion from his now dwindling income. From then onwards his travel adventures were purely in his imagination. In November 1898 he wrote a letter of resignation to the *Société de Géographie de Paris* in which he stated:

> I have reached the age at which it seems to me I should retire. Thus I am withdrawing little by little from all the Societies of which I have been a member for so many years and so I must resign my membership of the *Société de Géographie*, especially as I no longer go to Paris[1].

This was a significant letter, for during his career as an author, the *Société de Géographie* had been a crucial source of information and inspiration and a meeting place with some of the most eminent people of his generation. Some commentators have seen signs of increasing miserliness in the cancellation of subscriptions and other resignations. In the case of *La Société de Géographie*, which had meant so much to him and from which he would still regularly have received its journal and to which he had given important lectures, it seems more likely that his resignation was symbolic of a withdrawal from the past. Unable to visit Paris to hear lectures, and with his failing eyesight making reading the scientific papers difficult, resignation from the Society simply reflected his declining physical condition.

In spite of his poor health, Verne continued to assiduously honour his municipal obligations to Amiens, having been elected as a town councillor in 1888 and being re-elected twice subsequently. Verne was a Conservative in politics, perhaps with royalist sympathies, but joined the list of the Republican mayor in order to enhance his chances of election. Given his background, Verne was attached to the committee responsible for cultural activity. Moreover he had assumed other local responsibilities, as a Director of a savings bank, an honorary committee member of the Horticultural Society and election to the Amiens *Académie des Sciences, Belles Lettres et Arts*. He took an active interest in the theatre, music and inaugurated the magnificent Circus building. In general he lent his support to all aspects of modernisation of the town. This attachment to provincial affairs offered him both a diversion and an excuse. In reply to a letter from an editor requesting endorsement of a proposed new revue Verne replied:

> ... allow me to decline the honour of writing an introduction to this new publication; I now live too much in the province to give it the Parisian touch that it requires[2].

Verne's priority was to continue the production of manuscripts and he rejected invitations to contribute to other literature, which he regarded as unproductive and unremunerated. His absence from the academic resources that he had exploited in Paris was only a partial constraint. From the time of his decision to settle permanently in Amiens, Verne was a member of the town's *Société Industrielle*. This gave him access to the Society's library and each day, after five hours writing every morning followed by an early lunch, Verne would make his way to consult the journals and newspapers held there. If he had become a provincial by adoption, he was nevertheless generous with his time, devoted to interviews and greeting journalists and visitors graciously until his illness became terminal. The combination of health problems and loss of family and friends closest to him profoundly affected his literary mood. Whereas, with the partial exception of *Les Indes noires*, Verne's 'Scottish' novels had a positive touch and happy endings, new and often more gloomy themes now prevailed in much of his writing. Verne's memories of Scotland were full of exuberance, contact with his ancestral roots and were poised at the transition from Romanticism to Realism in European literature. His enthusiasm for Scotland and his enjoyment in creating Scottish characters in evocative settings fitted ill with his mood in his ageing years. This does not mean that his feelings for Scotland had diminished. On the contrary, in an interview with a journalist in the year before his death he recalled his 1879 visit to Scotland and the sensational effect that Fingal's Cave had on him and which led to the writing of *Le Rayon vert*.[3]

Although his fondness for Scotland remained intact, since his visit to America aboard the *Great Eastern* in 1867, the United States began to figure more prominently in his writing. As compared with the early years of his success when the heroes of his novels were predominantly British, including a significant proportion of Scots, in the 1870s Verne gave much greater prominence to Americans and his attitude to the English and its Empire became ever more critical. This was epitomised after his visit to Gibraltar in the *St-Michel III* in 1884. Having witnessed the apes on the Rock, he was moved to write a bitter and distinctly anti-British satire which he entitled *Gil Braltar* in which an uprising of the apes is suppressed by an extremely ugly Commanding General. The British retention of the colony is attributed by Verne to the appointment by the British of a series of ugly Commanding Generals recognised by the apes as their leader! No fewer than 23 of his novels take place entirely or partly in America. The use of Scotland as a setting seems to have been lost in his more general antipathy towards Britain. America on the other hand offered new literary horizons, for it was becoming increasingly clear that the advances in technology and modernity that Verne admired were now situated in the United States rather than Britain. Even so, his admiration of America was not unqualified. While admiring the energy of the new nation, as evinced in his early American novels, in his later novels it is manifest that the relentless search for wealth and materialism awoke Verne's increasing disdain of the greed. Ultimately, he saw the strength of the mighty dollar as inspiring the imperialist attitude that he had come to despise in the English. In fact Verne began to entertain ideas about the future which would not be out of place today. The future of the world's resources and their exploitation by unbridled capitalism concerned him. In one of his last novels, published in the year of his death, *L'invasion de la mer*, 1905, (*The Invasion of the Sea*), Verne describes a project of the French colonial power to flood part of the Tunisian Sahara desert by diverting sea water. The scheme is conceived without consideration of the environmental impact and without any reference to the wishes of the indigenous Tuareg population.

In spite of progressive infirmity, Verne continued to deliver manuscripts to Hetzel's son who had taken over his father's business. Indeed, at his death, he had accumulated a bank of unpublished manuscripts which appeared posthumously. However it is now known that his son Michel substantially amended some manuscripts and that he also published under his father's name work that was essentially his own.

Verne's health deteriorated rapidly in 1905 and on 24 March he succumbed to his battle against diabetes. In Scotland reaction to his death was mixed. *The Scotsman* seems merely to have reported his passing. By contrast *The Glasgow Herald* published on 25 March an obituary provided by a Reuter's correspondent filed from Amiens. It was on the whole a sympathetic and well-informed piece as the following extract shows:

> Although the dreamer entered largely into Verne's stories there was nevertheless an immense amount of genuine information and everything he wrote came to be regarded with a scientific as well as an imaginative interest. In appearance he was fairly stout, with silvery hair and beard, and restless brown eyes full of humour and kindness – an altogether commanding personality.

We can compare this with a particularly inept obituary in Glasgow's *Evening Times* of the same date:

> M. Jules Verne, who died yesterday at the advanced age of 77 was not a literary man. While his medium was fiction, he did not create any great characters, or write any novel for which we can prophesy permanence, or wield a style to secure for him the admiration of adult readers of cultured taste. During more than thirty years he made himself indispensable to that section of the reading public which is perhaps the most difficult to please. The Human Boy is perhaps the most exacting and the most honest of literary critics.

Admittedly the *Evening Times* was a 'popular' newspaper as compared with the *Glasgow Herald*, but its obituary indicates common perceptions of Verne. He was regarded in Britain as essentially a writer of science fiction and a children's author, and more specifically an author for boys. The fact that the obituary did not make reference to any of Verne's books suggests that the vast range of his novels was unknown to its author. The notion that Verne did not create any memorable characters suggests that the obituary writer was unfamiliar with Phileas Fogg or Captain Nemo, to name but the most obvious examples. Remarkably, neither of the Glasgow obituaries gives a mention of Verne's relationship to Scotland nor of the fact that he had twice visited the city. Certainly the *Evening Times* author would have won no prizes for prediction. To state that Verne was not 'a literary man' who 'did not create any great characters' and that 'one cannot prophesy any permanence' [for his novels] makes one wonder if he had actually read any books by the man who became the most translated French author of all time and who is in the top four or five translated authors worldwide. Even more disappointing was the obituary published in *The Glasgow Saturday Citizen* on 1 April 1905. This was quite a sophisticated weekly broadsheet with a strong emphasis on literature and a pronounced familiarity with French literature. In the weeks preceding Verne's death, for example, long essays had been published on Verlaine, Zola and George Sand. The obituary read;

> Jules Verne belonged to almost every country whose boys read. The great romancist [sic] was born in Nantes in 1828, so that at his death last week he was in his seventy eighth year. After vainly attempting to make a name for himself by writing plays, he abandoned dramatic for the Stock Exchange, but the study of finance brought him neither wealth nor celebrity, and it was only when he wrote 'Five Weeks in a Balloon' that he began to attract notice. One of his most famous books 'Round the world in Eighty Days' is said to have been suggested to him by the reading of a circular sent out by Messrs Thomas Cook and Sons. M. Verne's secret of production was the same as Sir Walter Scott's – early rising.

This obituary is consistent with others published in Scotland in considering that Verne was not a substantial author and that his readership was mainly of schoolboy age. Possibly this view was encouraged by the publication of some of his novels in serial form in *The Boy's Own Paper*[4]. Obituaries published in Scotland make no reference to the fact that Verne had lived through turbulent political times with several changes of regime. Nor is reference made to the fact that a man who abhorred violence experienced both conquest and occupation from external power and bloody uprisings internally. Verne's affection for Scotland and the creative inspiration that he drew from this must be juxtaposed against the political and social changes that he lived through in France. Politically, France abandoned the Orléans monarchy in the 1848 revolution leading to the creation of the Second Republic, which was not without extreme violence in the Paris uprising. Little more than 20 years later, the catastrophe of defeat in the Franco-Prussian War impinged directly on Verne. Northern France was occupied and his wife was obliged to accept German soldiers billeted on the Verne family house in Amiens. In protest against the humiliation of France, Paris once more erupted. Verne visited the city and witnessed at first hand the horrors of the commune uprising which was eventually suppressed with the loss of many thousands of lives. To Verne, whose political sympathy was to conservatism rather than republicanism, these events reinforced his hatred of violence.

Socially, several movements excited popular sentiment in the second half of the 19th century. Freemasonry lurked beneath the republican surface and Verne has been suspected, erroneously it would appear, of involvement in such subversive activity. Anti-clericalism also thrived under the concern that the Church could wield indirect political opposition to a secular State. More seriously, antisemitism flourished in certain sections of society and critics have considered that Verne's portrayal of Jewish characters demonstrates a less than sympathetic attitude. Antisemitism in France reached a crescendo in the Dreyfus Affair, when an army officer was convicted, cashiered and imprisoned on a charge of spying for the Germans as a result of falsified evidence. Verne initially joined the camp of the anti-Drefuysards, again an attitude which has been advanced as a further instance of antisemitism on his part. Such a claim is almost certainly exaggerated and it could be argued that Verne was simply reflecting in his writing in this, and other respects, the prevailing social and political tensions of his time.

In fact, we find only tinges of this turbulence in Verne's Scottish novels. Rather they manifest his preference for political stability, hierarchical social order and a progression towards modernity rather than revolutionary disruption. Viewed in this perspective, the Scottish novels betray almost an escapist approach in which the trauma and tumult inside France, and to a degree in his personal life, are sublimated in the romantic notions of Scotland that he had held since his youth. If we consider the main characters in the novels then the dominant quality is orthodoxy and respectability, enshrined in the aristocracy in the case of Lord Glenarvan or the middle classes in James Starr, the Melvill brothers or James Playfair. The communal spirit of the population of Coal City is an expression of peaceful solidarity and a far cry from the horror of the commune of Paris. The irrepressible Jack Ryan is the least stereotypical of Verne's Scottish creations, but provides him with a vehicle to indulge his fascination with legends and the supernatural. It is true that disturbing social themes are invoked in the novels and in particular the iniquity of slavery and the brutality of colonialism, and the reverse side of progress in industrial technology is reflected in his depictions of urban poverty. Verne's condemnation of wealth and greed is personified in the Reverend Tyrcomel, although this reflects in exaggerated form his own sentiments in later life rather than an explicit condemnation of a Scottish shortcoming.

It can be argued that by standing aside from the dramatic events in France that punctuated his life, Verne was not only indulging in escapism based on romanticism, further enhanced by his first hand experience of Scotland, but that he also gave himself the time and space to create his favourite literary genre, the 'geographical' novel.

Finale

For all that by the time of his death Jules Verne was world famous, there is still much about him that is not known or is unexplained. Numerous biographies of varying reliability have not completely clarified a life in which there are gaps of knowledge and contradictions in interpretation. Outside his group of closest friends and relatives Verne was a very private person and much of his personal life remains shrouded in mystery. Certainty is not aided by the fact that he destroyed mountains of letters and personal files in 1898 as a result bickering within the extended Verne family. Many documents in the possession of family members appear to have remained concealed from the public gaze, intentionally or otherwise. Inevitably an aura of speculation therefore surrounds sensitive aspects of his life, including theories concerning his sexuality and the expression of this in his literature. Gradually, new discoveries and insights emerge, for example the very recent suggestion that he may have had an illegitimate child. Little of this ambiguity attaches to his affection for Scotland, nor to his appreciation of Scottish literature. Certain critics see a homosexual relationship between the Melvill brothers in *The Green Ray*, strengthened by the orphan Helena's reference to them as father and mother respectively. If Verne intended this interpretation then there is no obvious further stereotyping of their relationship to encourage this theory in detail. Similarly, sexual innuendo has been attached to the penetration of Fingal's Cave by Sinclair to rescue Helena. Such a psychological interpretation of an event, the setting of which Verne had seen and which had impressed him so deeply, does not seem indispensable to an appreciation of the dramatic event. It must be recalled that Hetzel viewed the *Voyages Extraordinaires* as improving stories for the very young and as suitable for consumption by predominantly middle-class adults. In such circumstances explicit references of a sexual nature would have been inappropriate. Undoubtedly there are political and social undertones in *The Underground City* but we now know that the novel was heavily amended at Hetzel's demand and this has obscured and considerably toned down Verne's original message.

The fact remains that Verne has produced tales set in Scotland that stand on their own merits as novels which can be perfectly well appreciated by the vast majority of readers at face value. Significantly, except for *The Fabulous Adventures of Master Antifer*, which only has an episode in Scotland, all the other four novels end in joyous weddings, although it is now known that to a significant degree this reflected Hetzel's preference for happy and non-controversial endings rather than any sentimentality on the part of Verne, given that his own marriage had been less than fulfilling. It is strange that Scotland, a country that takes immense pride in the Auld Alliance with France, and which still values highly its cultural, sporting and commercial links, should have such little awareness of the Scottish connection with France's most widely read and translated author. It is hoped that, however modestly, this book will help redress this omission.

Notes

1   *Bibliothèque Nationale de Paris, Section Cartes et Plans, colis No 14*, (2502).

2   Taylor Institute Library, Oxford University, Archive MS.F/Verne 3.

3   Interview with Gordon Jones, 'Jules Verne at Home', *Temple Bar*, 129, 1904, 664–671.

4   Of the large number of translated Verne novels that this author has collected in second hand bookshops in the Glasgow area, the vast majority are

inscribed as being school prizes or are Christmas or birthday presents. Without exception, the personal dedications indicate that the recipients were boys. An Edinburgh bookseller advertising in *The Scotsman* in December 1875, conveniently for the Christmas present market, announced the availability in *The Youth's Library of Wonders and Adventures* of four new Verne novels, adding 'Every boy should read these startling stories by Jules Verne'!

Reading on

THIS BOOK HAS SIMPLY examined the personal and creative relationship between Jules Verne and Scotland. It has not attempted to be a comprehensive biographical portrait of a man as complex and often as misrepresented as Jules Verne. Even less has it pretensions to be a work of literary criticism. Fortunately both of these tasks have recently been addressed by two British authorities. William Butcher's book, *Jules Verne. The Definitive Biography*, Thunder's Mouth Press, New York, 2006, Second Edition, 2008, is a highly detailed biography. Exploiting new documentary evidence, it produces a picture of Verne, warts and all. Here we see a man not averse to plagiarism, putting his name to work which was not entirely his own, a neglectful husband and father, almost certainly an adulterer and yet a tower of imaginative fiction which has entranced generations of young people and adults alike. Timothy Unwin's *Jules Verne: Journeys in Writing*, Liverpool University Press, 2005, is a critical analysis of Verne's oeuvre and includes new interpretations of his work. Together these two books give a comprehensive picture of Jules Verne, with extensive bibliographies of works in both French and English permit the serious scholar to probe in depth the life and literature of this extraordinary author.

In addition, Herbert R Lottman's *Jules Verne: An exploratory biography*, St Martin's Press, New York, 1996, provides an American appreciation of Verne. This is significant in that interest in Verne's life and works is particularly strong in the United States and the majority of his novels have appeared there in translation. Unfortunately the two Scottish journeys are only treated in brief outline. Two well known French Verne biographers have had their works translated into English and although no longer in print are commonly able to be purchased second hand from online booksellers. *Jules Verne*, Staples Press, London, 1954, is a translation of the biography published by a distant relative of Verne, Marguerite Allotte de la Fuÿe. In fact her preferred appellation as Verne's niece exaggerated her true status. She married a great nephew of Verne's wife and therefore in the absence of a blood relationship was only entitled to the status of 'great niece-in-law'. Nevertheless, this Verne connection added an undeserved authenticity to her biography. Her chronology of

Verne's Scottish travels and novels is unsound. This is an unreliable biography given the author's tendency to romanticise and even invent incidents in Verne's life and thus to perpetuate myths concerning his early life in particular in later biographies. *Jules Verne, a Biography*, by Verne's grandson, Jean-Jules Verne, Macdonald and Jane's, London, 1976, is a less imaginative and more reliable biography with interesting illustrations but is nevertheless somewhat dated in view of subsequent discoveries.

Probably a major reason why Jules Verne's relationship to Scotland is not more widely known is that only three of his 'Scottish' novels have appeared in recent English translations. *The Underground City* (2005) translated by Sarah Crozier, and *The Green Ray* (2009) and *The Blockade Runners* (2011), both translated by Karen Loukes, have been published by Luath Press, Edinburgh, and replace earlier and less authentic translations. Both versions include the evocative original illustrations of the Hetzel editions and also have brief contextual essays. A translation of *Voyage à Reculons en Angleterre et en Ecosse* as *Backwards to Britain* was published by Chambers, Edinburgh in 1992. Currently unavailable in bookshops, it can be found at times second hand or can be ordered as new from the residual holder of the stock, William Butcher (wbutcher@netvigator.com). This is a crucial source not only for its comedic content and as the only detail of his 1859 visit, but because it reveals much of the young Verne and it foreshadows the blending of geography and history which was to be characteristic of the *Voyages Extraordinaires*.

The National Library of Scotland has a stock of almost 400 books by or about Verne. This valuable collection suffers from some of the limitations already mentioned. There are multiple copies of the best known novels, most of the books are translations including many produced during the 19th or early 20th century and suffer from errors, omissions or over simplification to make the stories accessible to children. There are, nevertheless, a number of early French edition volumes published by Hetzel including *Le Rayon vert* and *Les Indes noires*. The full list of Verne holdings can be consulted on the National Library of Scotland's online catalogue. For many readers, the most convenient sources of the 'Scottish' novels in English will be electronic, although the quality and completeness of such translations is variable. The website created with the utmost dedication by the late Zvi Har' El and maintained by his son includes links to English translations of all but one of the 'Scottish' novels. All of the alternative translations, including those under the auspices of Project Gutenberg, can be accessed free of charge. The home page address for this source, and for an enormous amount of information on Verne is Zvi Har'El's Jules Verne Collection (www.jv.gilead.org.il). *The Fabulous Adventures of Master Antifer* remains un-translated in an authentic edition since the end of the 19th century.

Apart from the archival evidence cited in the Notes, the vast majority of the material exploited in the preparation of the present book is inevitably of a secondary nature under the generic heading of the local history and geography of 19th century Scotland. This poses particular problems since although there is an abundance of background material in book form, many of the most rewarding and informative sources consist of pamphlets and other ephemera not generally available except in research collections in public and university libraries, or, with good fortune, in second hand bookshops. Accordingly the material listed below includes only sources likely to be available commercially or in the collections of major libraries.

Maps and Atlases

Jules Verne claimed that it was the study of maps, globes and atlases that inspired him to write his 'geographical' novels. Reference to cartographic sources greatly enhances an appreciation of his Scottish travels and novels. *The National Gazeteer of Great Britain and Ireland,* published in 1868, has been used in the construction of most of the maps in this book. This atlas, with sheets devoted to each of the Scottish counties, is a good reference point, especially for transport systems. For local detail, the first editions of the Ordnance Survey permit a detailed reconstruction of Verne's local travel. In the case of Edinburgh and Glasgow modern reproductions of these maps at a larger scale are available commercially from The Godfrey Edition, Consett, DH8 7PW, the individual sheets including useful descriptive text of the area depicted.

19th and early 20th Century Guidebooks

It is known that Verne made extensive use of guidebooks in French and French translations of English language travel guides. Guidebooks in

English are very useful, not only as a source of town maps, but help to identify the detail mentioned by Verne. In particular detailed town plans, listings of hotels, and in some cases details of rail, steamer and coach timetables, make a reconstruction of Verne's travels relatively straight-forward. Excellent examples are Ward Lock's frequently revised *Illustrated Guide Books,* in which the volumes on Edinburgh, Glasgow and Oban cover the areas visited by Verne. The *Thorough Guides,* published by Dulau and Company, London, contain an astonishing amount of detail, based on itineraries and including coloured maps by Bartholomew, the Edinburgh cartography company. *The Guide to Scotland, Part One,* by MJB Baddeley, covers all the relevant ground. A rather more condensed guide, *Murray's Handbook for Travellers in Scotland,* is also based on routes and has an emphasis on history and architecture to a greater extent than landscape.

A charming little volume with abundant line drawings is *Tweed's Guide to Glasgow and the Clyde* first published in 1872. It was reprinted by The Molindinar Press, Glasgow, in 1972 in two volumes.

A further guide whose charm is enhanced by the fine reproduced prints is *Black's Picturesque Tourist of Scotland*, which was the subject of revised editions during the 19th century. In her diary entry for 2 September 1869, Queen Victoria wrote of her sail along Loch Katrine, 'We had several guide-books, of which we find Black's far the best'. The editions for 1857 and for 1883 are the most appropriate for use in connection with Verne's two visits.

Pictorial Resources

An abundance of well illustrated books on 19th century Scotland exists but this can be complemented by comprehensive photographic collections in the public domain, some of which can be examined online. The Edinburgh Central Library has a collection of over 100,000 images con-sisting of paintings and early photographs. A large sample of these can be examined online by reference to the site Capital Collections. For Glasgow, the Mitchell Library website has a consultable collection of images of the city and the Clyde under the rubric Virtual Mitchell. Two major special collections, the Wotherspoon and the Langmuir collections, portraying transport images, especially of shipping, are housed in the library. Shipping scenes on the Lower Clyde are prominent in the pictorial collections of the Watt Library and the Maclean Art Gallery and Museum in Greenock and a selection can be viewed in an online catalogue.

Other public libraries, as at Dumbarton, Stirling and the Carnegie Library in Dunfermline, have photograph collections. A particularly important collection of archives and photographs is the Mclean Collection of Scottish Railway History housed in the William Patrick Library in Kirkintilloch. In addition to the above public collections, other pictorial resources are available in the commercial sector. For example, the classic collection of photographs of Old Glasgow by Thomas Annan is maintained for consultation and purchase at the Annan Gallery in Glasgow. The University of Aberdeen houses the George Washington Wilson Collection. This is an enormous collection of 19th century photographs. The catalogue can be consulted online including thumbnail images. While Verne wrote some fine descriptive passages in his Scottish novels, reference to the illustrative material indicated above enhances an appreciation of the scenes which both delighted and shocked him in his journeys.

Newspapers and Magazines

The National Library of Scotland has archival collections of virtually every significant Scottish newspaper and magazine, many of which are no longer published. The list is itemised under the heading Newsplan Scotland on the Library's website. The Mitchell Library in Glasgow has a comprehensive archive collection of the city's newspapers in the 19th century. Direct references to Verne are of course not extensive and the search via microform is time consuming. Indirectly however, newspapers give a magnificent background source for the period of Verne's travels in Scotland. Details of shipping, hotel accommodation, weather and sea conditions and much other local detail can be found in articles or advertisements. Remarkably, even local papers, for example the *Oban Telegraph,* provide a wealth of detail at the local scale and beyond and are a testimony to the curiosity and educational standard of the readership even in relatively remote predominantly rural areas of Scotland.

The Third Statistical Accounts of Scotland

In spite of their title, the *Third Statistical Accounts* are primarily texts, illustrated with some statistical data. These are substantial volumes, based on counties and cities, extending up to 1,000 pages each. Although published in the 1950s and 1960s, substantial chapters are devoted in each volume to geology, geography, climate and economic history. The history of transport features prominently as do the traditional industries witnessed by Verne. They are a valuable source of background information relevant to Verne's Scottish travels and writing and can be consulted at municipal and county libraries in Scotland. In the preparation of this book reference has been made to the Statistical Accounts of Edinburgh City, Glasgow City, and to the counties of Fife, Stirling, Argyll and Perth and Kinross.

Local History Societies

A wealth of local history societies, too numerous to mention, exist in Central Scotland, many of which produce journals and magazines. In particular transport is well represented with specialist societies on railway, canal and maritime history. Of particular relevance are The Ships of Calmac Society and The Caledonian Railway Association. Place Name Societies also provide valuable local information on places visited by Verne. Many such local societies maintain web pages and are generous in answering enquiries.

For the Pilgrim

If there is no physical commemoration of Verne's connection with the nation to be found in Scotland, the same is obviously not true of France. Two places in particular are magnets for the enthusiast, his place of birth, Nantes, and his adoptive town, Amiens in Picardy. For those wishing to extend their knowledge of Verne the man and his works beyond the scope of the present book, a pilgrimage to these two centres is a rewarding experience, especially for francophones.

The city of Nantes is understandably proud of its native son and this is expressed in several ways. For the scholar, the Centre d'Etudes verniennes, houses the most important collection of original Verne manuscripts, acquired by donations and by purchase on the part of the municipality. Over 5,000 documents are housed in this branch of the Municipal Library and Verne's handwritten manuscripts are accessible online. Secondly, a Jules Verne Trail has been established and an excellent brochure guide has been produced by the tourist section of the *Mairie*. In the space of a couple of hours, the trail encompasses the significant sites and buildings in Verne's life from the city centre to the former Verne family rural retreat of Chantenay, with the high spot being a handsome building holding the Jules Verne Museum. Overlooking the river and docks of the Loire, beloved of the juvenile Verne, the museum houses a priceless collection of documents and memorabilia. Details of both the Centre d'Etudes verniennes and the Musée Jules Verne can be accessed via the website www.nantes.fr/julesverne, including online original manuscripts by following the link *Les Collections*.

Amiens

If Nantes has its rich manuscript collection and Verne trail, the most evocative survival of Verne is to be found in Amiens. Between 1882 and 1900 Verne lived in the Maison de la Tour, a four storey house surmounted by a circular tower and with an enclosed garden, located at 2, Rue Charles Dubois, approximately a kilometre from the town centre (www.jules-verne.net). In a simple study, doubling as a bedroom, overlooking the railway line from Amiens to Boulogne, with the massive cathedral on the skyline, Verne wrote 34 novels. After a varied history, the house was acquired by the Amiens town council in 1980, transformed into a museum and opened to the public in 1991. In 2006, a year after the centenary of Verne's death, the building was reopened after major renovations and refurbishment. Moreover, by this time the town council had purchased the major collection of books, documents, furniture and other items from the great Italian Verne collector Count Piero Gondolo della Riva. Many of these objects are displayed in the Maison de la Tour and the presence of Verne is almost tangible. Within a short distance of this museum, the municipal library houses this major Verne collection including the above purchase, and organises periodic events and exhibitions. Critically, the *carnets de voyages*, Verne's log of his voyages in the *St-Michel* III, for so long absent from public gaze, can be viewed. Also

Objectif Lacour-Berthiot — Plaques Supra
600. Tombeau de Jules Verne
Au Cimetière de la Madeleine, à AMIENS
C. Boulanger, Entrepreneur   Albert Roze, Statuaire   E. Douillet, Architecte

The tomb of Jules Verne in Amiens.
The inscription reads 'Onwards towards
immortality and eternal youth'.

Anonymous postcard

in Amiens is the Centre International Jules Verne. This is an important academic and documentary resource centre which also publishes an important series of monographs, organises conferences and excursions and is a repository of editions of Verne's books and biographical works.

The most emotional monument in Amiens is Verne's tomb in the Cemetery of the Madeleine. Here Verne is interred along with his wife Honorine. The tomb has an evocative statue of Verne raising the lid of his tomb and bears the inscription 'Onward to Immortality and Eternal Youth'. In the public gardens close to La Maison Jules Verne is situated a bust of Verne overlooking three children reading avidly. It was inaugurated in 1905, the year of his death.

Paris

The French National Library, *La Bibliothèque Nationale* in Paris has a very large collection of Verne's publications together with journals and works of criticism in French. The volumes in the *Voyages Extraordinaires* series can be downloaded by reference to the website of digital reproductions at www.gallica2.bnf.fr.

Yverdon-les–Bains, Switzerland. Espace Jules Verne

The most recent research resource results from the donation of the collection of a Swiss-American, Jean-Michel Margot to Yverdon-les Bains. The collection consists of 20,000 items, books, documents and memorabilia, collected over a period of 50 years. It is housed in the Espace Jules Verne, a specially constructed annexe to the town's science fiction museum, La Maison d'Ailleurs, and the highlight is a mouth-watering collection of Hetzel editions.

Journals Devoted to Verne Studies

The primary academic journal of Verne research is the *Bulletin de la Société Jules Verne*, published in French in Paris.

La Revue Jules Verne, has been published in French by the Centre International Jules Verne in Amiens. Over 28 issues have been published since 1996, and consist of monographs, themed essay collections, interviews, discussions and book reviews.

The North American Jules Verne Society produces a newsletter in English entitled *The Extraordinary Voyages*. A recent innovation is an electronic journal of peer reviewed articles and news items available free of subscription and downloadable entitled *Verniana* (www.verniana.org).

Index

Some other books published by **LUATH** PRESS

The Underground City, a novel set in Scotland

Jules Verne
Translated by Sarah Crozier, with a foreword by Professor Ian Thompson
ISBN 978 1842820 80 3 PBK £7.99

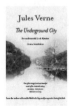

Ten years after manager James Starr left the Aberfoyle mine underneath Loch Katrine exhausted of coal, he receives an intriguing missive that suggests that the pit isn't barren after all. When Starr returns and discovers that there is indeed more coal to quarry, he and his workers are beset by strange events, hinting at a presence that does not wish to see them excavate the cavern further.

Could there be someone out to sabotage their work? Someone with a grudge against them? Or is something more menacing afoot, something supernatural that they cannot see or understand? When one of his miners falls in love with a young girl found abandoned down a mineshaft, their unknown assailant makes it clear that nothing will stop its efforts to shut down the mine, even if it means draining Loch Katrine itself!

The Green Ray

Jules Verne
Translated by Karen Loukes, with an afterword by Professor Ian Thompson
ISBN 978 1905222 12 4 PBK £7.99

The green ray – a beam of green light seen at the horizon at the setting of the sun – is a phenomenon that is well known to sailors, who are often able to see it over the edge of the ocean. When a newspaper article tells Helena Campbell, whose impending arranged marriage is less than a love match, that seeing the green ray is an indication of true love, she refuses to marry anyone until she has seen it. Her quest to view the green ray takes her on an island-hopping tour of the Hebrides that nearly costs her her life, and Helena must ask herself – is seeing the green ray worth it? With which of her suitors will Helena see the ray? Will she ever see it at all?

Coming soon:

The Blockade Runners

Jules Verne
Translated by Karen Loukes, with an afterword by Professor Ian Thompson
ISBN 978 1905222 20 9 PBK £6.99

Set during the American Civil War, Verne's iconic story travels across the Atlantic into a turbulent period in history, where man's capabilities and the extent he will go for love are put to the test.

Details of these and other books published by Luath Press can be found at:

www.luath.co.uk

Luath Press Limited
committed to publishing well written books worth reading

LUATH PRESS takes its name from Robert Burns, whose little collie Luath (*Gael.*, swift or nimble) tripped up Jean Armour at a wedding and gave him the chance to speak to the woman who was to be his wife and the abiding love of his life. Burns called one of 'The Twa Dogs' Luath after Cuchullin's hunting dog in Ossian's *Fingal*. Luath Press was established in 1981 in the heart of Burns country, and now resides a few steps up the road from Burns' first lodgings on Edinburgh's Royal Mile.
Luath offers you distinctive writing with a hint of unexpected pleasures.

Most bookshops in the UK, the US, Canada, Australia, New Zealand and parts of Europe either carry our books in stock or can order them for you. To order direct from us, please send a £sterling cheque, postal order, international money order or your credit card details (number, address of cardholder and expiry date) to us at the address below. Please add post and packing as follows: UK – £1.00 per delivery address; overseas surface mail – £2.50 per delivery address; overseas airmail – £3.50 for the first book to each delivery address, plus £1.00 for each additional book by airmail to the same address. If your order is a gift, we will happily enclose your card or message at no extra charge.

Luath Press Limited
543/2 Castlehill
The Royal Mile
Edinburgh EH1 2ND
Scotland

Telephone: 0131 225 4326 (24 hours)
Fax: 0131 225 4324
email: sales@luath.co.uk
Website: www.luath.co.uk

ILLUSTRATION: IAN KELLAS